FALLING THROUGH SPACE

Falling Through Space

The Journals of Ellen Gilchrist

UNIVERSITY PRESS OF MISSISSIPPI / JACKSON

www.upress.state.ms.us

First published by Little, Brown & Company in 1987.

Permissions to quote from copyrighted material appear on page 224.

08 07 06 05 04 03 02 01 00   4 3 2 1

Library of Congress Cataloging-in-Publication Data

Gilchrist, Ellen, 1935–
   Falling through space : the journals of Ellen Gilchrist.
     p. cm.
   "Banner books."
   Originally published: Boston: Little, Brown and Co., 1987.
   ISBN 1-57806-291-8 (pbk. : alk. paper)
    1. Gilchrist, Ellen, 1935– 2. Gilchrist, Ellen, 1935– —Homes and
haunts—Mississippi. 3. Authors, American—20th century—Biography.
4. Mississippi—Social life and customs. 5. Plantation life—Mississippi.
6. Authorship. I. Title.

   PS3557.I34258 Z465 2000
   813'.54—dc21
   [B]

00-027340

British Library Cataloging-in-Publication Data available

FOR MARSHALL AND ELLEN AND AURORA

The Wu Li Masters know that "science" and "religion" are only dances, and that those who follow them are dancers. The dancers may claim to follow "truth" or claim to seek "reality" but the Wu Li Masters know better. They know that the true love of all dancers is dancing.

—GARY ZUKAV from *The Dancing Wu Li Masters*

Contents

Origins

*T*HIS is my home. This is where I was born. This is the bayou that runs in my dreams, this is the bayou bank that taught me to love water, where I spent endless summer hours alone or with my cousins. This is where I learned to swim, where mud first oozed up between my toes. This is where I saw embryos inside the abdomens of minnows. This is where I believed that if I was vain and looked too long into the water I would turn into a flower.

This is where I learned the legend of the greedy dog. There was an old dog on a raft and he had a bone in his teeth and he looked down into the water and saw a dog carrying a bone and he dropped the one he was holding to snatch the other dog's bone away and so lost both bones, the real and the imaginary.

That's a new bridge. The one that was here when I was small had a beautiful elaborate scaffolding on top. I thought I must be a princess, of royal blood, to have such a bridge with such a magnificent top. To have such land with so many bugs and a bayou with so many fish and mussels and gars and maybe even alligators.

This is the porch that at one time ran all the way around the house. My grandfather built this house and my mother came here when she was four years old. My brother was born in that front bedroom. I was born forty miles away in a hospital and only came here three days later.

The ghost of Eli Nailor walks these halls. He was a black boy who was adopted by my great-great-grandmother when he was orphaned as a child. The woman I am named for raised him. He was the cook in this house all the days of his life and had a cabin beside the kitchen and the gardens and the henhouse and the chickenyard.

This was a good life. There were never slaves here. The black people came here after the Civil War; they were free people from Natchez. Black people and white people lived and worked here in harmony. My grandfather thought of himself as an Englishman. He was tall and proud and brave and civilized.

Here is where my Aunt Roberta raised angora rabbits during the Second World War and there is the chickenhouse where I spied on the Broad Jump Pit when my brother and my cousins were training for the Olympics.

This is the richest land in the world. The topsoil goes thirteen to eighteen feet in some places. You could grow anything here. We grew cotton. We grow soybeans also now. My godfather, Coon Wade, farms this land. He was my grandfather's friend. He serves that friendship still.

This is my world, where I was formed, where I came from, who I am. This is where my sandpile was. I have spent a thousand hours alone beneath this tree making forts for the fairies to dance on in the moonlight. At night, after I was asleep, my mother would come out here and dance her fingers all over my sand forts so that in the morning I would see the prints and believe that fairies danced at night in the sand.

This is where the barn used to be. There was a black stallion here that we called the Count of Monte Christo and mules so mean they could scare you out of riding them.

This is Ditty's cabin. She was as straight and tall as a tree, half black and half white. She told the other black people what to do. She was the mother of Mark and Inez and Man. I would come here and ask permission to come in and she would grant it and I would step over the wooden doorframe to the dirt floor. I would sit on her bed, on her spotless quilts, and eat cornbread and gossip about everything that was going on.

Then I would go to the store and play the slot machine and

sell snuff and drink cold sweet drinks and eat pork and beans out of a can. Life is not supposed to be simple but it seemed simple to me. It was get up in the morning and be happy. It was go out in the yard and lie down on the ground and listen to China.

This is the levee. This is what keeps the Mississippi River within its banks. My father helped build this levee. I was conceived in a levee camp in a huge green tent from the Memphis tent company. In those photographs my mother is always wearing jodhpurs.

Before the white man came the Indians built mounds to get on when the water rose. Before even the Cherokees came the Mound Builders were here.

This is the Indian mound with a house built on top where my grandparents spent the first year of their marriage. There are other mounds on Hopedale Plantation. My great-grandmother forbade us to dig in them as they were sacred burial places. It was the only thing I ever remember Babbie forbidding us to do.

This was my great-great-grandmother's room. She lived until I was four in perfect health. When they used such things she would spend the late summer in this room sewing together the long white cotton bags the black people dragged behind them to pick the cotton.

These are the catfish ponds that take the place of cattle. Flying over my home I am appalled at how much of the land has been turned into catfish ponds. Things change. The only constant is change. There is nothing to fear. The land is its own God. It will heal itself if it needs to.

I could never live in a city. I need to smell the earth. I need to be here when it storms. At night when I was small great rainstorms would come swooping down across the Delta, tearing down the light poles and the telephone poles. My grandfather loved inventions. As soon as they invented the telephone he and his fellow planters met in Grace and arranged to have telephones. Then each of them cut down trees and strung wire and the wires met at the Grace post office and hooked up there to go to Rolling Fork and on to Greenville.

This is Greenfields' cemetery. This is where my mother's people are buried. Stewart Floyd Alford and Nell Biggs Alford and Margaret Connell and Ellen Martin and so forth and so on. My cousins and my friends.

I wish they had lived forever. This country was made by pioneers. They probably could not have imagined us, our numbers and our terrible problems, our crowded cities and wonderful medicines and bitter endless feuds. What will be happening fifty years from now that I cannot imagine? What will my great-great-grandchildren think of me when they walk in my house and read my books? When they try to piece together my life from my photographs and my legends.

℞

THE ROAD to the store led past a line of pecan trees that looked down into the river. Swarms of gnats would come up out of nowhere and attack my face if I was stupid enough to walk there in the early morning or late afternoon. In the middle of the day the sun held them hostage on the bayou bank and I could walk along kicking the gravel with my sandals or stopping to pull up a dandelion or examine a rock or pause to feel my nickel in my pocket to make sure it was still there. Behind me Nailor and Baby Doll and Overflow and Henrietta were lined up on the porch stairs watching my progress. In front of me the people sitting on the benches outside the store were already thinking of things to say to me. "Good morning, little missy, how you do today?" "Look out, here she comes, the girl that sells the snuff. How much you going to charge today for all your bags and cans?" "How about giving a few cans away?" "Look out for that dog. He's the king of fleas."

It was talk like music and it meant they liked me and thought that I was funny. I liked them too. I didn't have enough sense to know what it meant to be black. It never occurred to me that they might want to do a single thing they weren't already doing.

"I'm not putting this nickel in that hell-damn old slot machine today," I'd say, and go straight inside and stick it in and pull the handle. Two oranges and a bar. Three nickels for one. I stuck them in as fast as I could pull the handle. Then turned to my cousin Cincinnatus to see what he had for me to do.

"Lost your nickel already," he said, giggling from behind the cash register.

"I won three the first time," I answered. Yang and yin. I already knew the outcome was not the whole story of anything. I knew the end contains the beginning. In the strange way that children know everything because they forget nothing, I knew that the loss of a nickel to the judgment of the slot machine was nothing really, was only a way to get the damn smelly thing out of my hand. What was a nickel in the scheme of things? Buffalo on one side, White House on the other, made your hand smell funny to hold it and if you swallowed it you were dead. My uncle Robert had a framed picture in his doctor's office of all the things children had swallowed that he had retrieved. An open safety pin was the only one that really caught my eye.

So the nickel was gone as so many had gone before it and I was no less than I had been and still had the walk to the store, still had long cool baths in the tub that had been made especially for my grandfather, who was six feet four inches

tall. A little girl could swim in that tub, could lie down and
drown if no one was watching, but they were always
watching, standing by with a hairbrush in their hands or
sitting on a little stool and dripping water onto my back or
begging me to let them wash my hair.

Dried with a big soft towel and carried down the hall and
dressed in one of the beautiful soft cotton dresses they were
always making me. My great-great-grandmother had been a
milliner in Philadelphia and the women in that house were
great artists of fashion and style and beauty. The clothes I
wore when I was a child have spoiled me for life. At great
collections in Paris or New York I turn up my nose at messy
hems or anything that isn't French seamed or smocked by
hand. When people ask me why there were so few women
artists in the past, I tell them it's because their definition of
artist is too narrow. I have worn dresses that should have won
a Nobel. "Let me see that dress," everyone at the store would
say. "Look here, Iris, see this dress Miss Babbie made this
child." And their fingers would explore the rickrack or
three-inch hem or perfectly fitted sleeves or smocking. Those
artists did not have to wait for some stranger in New York to
overcome his or her fear and say, Oh, yes, this is a nice piece
of work. The audience and critics were right there in the
room waiting for the last whir of the sewing machine and the
moment when the dress would come down from the sewing
table and be held up for inspection. What a life, with the sun
pouring down outside on the richest land in the world. THE
RICHEST LAND IN THE WORLD and we were happy
there. The black people and white people worked together
and spoke their grievances and only sickness or death or rain
in September could make us sad. The days were long in that
land of happy days and part of me lives there still.

A writer once said that a walk becomes a journey when
there is a destination. I had a destination every afternoon
when I was small. I would walk from the house to the store
and if my nickel had to be sacrificed to my greed that was
only one more gnat or interesting rock or possibly useful leaf.

℘

THE HARDEST THING to get hold of in the world is the truth; the easiest to keep once you capture it, once you know it plain. So I believe, but then I can't stand secrets. I want all the cards on the table. I want to know what's going on.

When I was a child I lived in a world of great order and politeness. "So polite," I once wrote, "that no one ever told the truth about anything." That was a cruel thing to write about a world as gentle and full of goodness as Hopedale Plantation. The grown people *were* elaborately and beautifully truthful about the surface of life, details, business arrangements, promises made and kept, appointments honored, facts kept straight. A man's word was his pledge in that world, his good name the dearest treasure of his life. Still, about the dark underside of life, birth and death, sex and the river, power and the wielding of power, God and the sky, these things stayed behind a levee of polite speaking and polite behavior. Why, when I was a child, did a certain pecan tree on the front lawn seem to have the greatest shadows and why was I the only one that ever played on the flagstone terrace beneath its branches or swung in its dusty web-covered swing? The grownups stayed away from that tree. With the great intuitive knowledge of children I knew I had that tree to myself. My cousins never played there. Even the wooden picnic table was never used and I would line up pecans upon its surface and make roads with them. The swing the rest of them used was one that swung out over the banks of the bayou. It was a nice swing also and anchored to a huge live oak tree, but no nicer than the pecan tree swing. As I said, I had that one to myself.

Many years later, on a cold fall day in Jackson, Mississippi, sitting in a car with my cousin, late in the afternoon, with the sun almost gone from the sky, I began to talk about that tree.

"It's still mysterious. And lonely. I went down there with a film crew last month and they felt it. The land is so alive down there."

"Perhaps it was the suicide?"

"What suicide?"

"A woman killed herself there. On that patio. Didn't you know about that?"

"Who killed herself? What woman?"

"Someone they knew. She had cancer and she wouldn't take whiskey for the pain. Nailor told me. She wouldn't take whiskey or any kind of dope and so she killed herself instead. At night beneath that tree."

"My God, the things that happened."

"I never would go near that tree after Nailor told me that."

"I wonder why no one ever told me?"

"Because you never listened. You were always talking."

"That's a nice thing to say."

"Well, it's true."

So the mystery was solved. And other mysteries open before me. A mysterious world, only fifty years away. Medical science was hard to practice when there were no drugs, no real hope to offer. My great-uncle was the only doctor in the county. He worked all day and read all night to keep up with the advances in medical science. But there was little he could do about things like cancer. When I first saw Eugene Smith's beautiful photographic essay, "Country Doctor," I thought of Uncle Robert and wept for the mastery and courage of his life. I should have wept for the time he had to waste trying to give me typhoid shots. It would take hours of pleading to get me to stick out my arm and hold still. Hours of pleading and promises and sticks of peppermint candy and being allowed to look at the skeleton in his closet. Afterwards I would have to be put to bed for the afternoon to recover from the trauma. I wonder what he did to recover from putting up with me.

The other great secret they kept from us was about sex. Whatever the animals did in the fields had nothing to do with what the white people did in the houses. The white people and beautiful tall sober black people who helped my grandfather run the place. *Nigger* was the word they used for black people who lived like animals. Nice people got married and were faithful and brought well-loved children into the world. At great danger to themselves women bore live children into the world that the world of men might live.

The graveyard around the little Episcopal church at Greenfields was littered with small tombstones that marked the graves of infants and children. It was hard to keep children alive in a land of mosquito-borne diseases. Children were bundled up and kept inside and watched over and guarded like diamonds. They were diamonds, black and white alike. Babies, new hope for the world, new voices in the clear blue air. Lambs were born in the pasture and colts and piglets and chickens hatched in the chickenyard and butterflies emerged from the cocoons we collected in the barn and calves dropped and all things multiplied and were fruitful in that rich fruitful land. Still, the birth of children was a thing apart. They were sent by God. Delivered by storks.

When I was nineteen years old, after having read thousands of books, on the night before I ran away to get married in the hills of north Georgia I sat up all night reading a book about how to have sexual intercourse. It was a book I had bought that afternoon at Rich's department store in Atlanta. I bought a white piqué dress with tiny pearl buttons all the way down the front. A white silk nightgown and robe, some white high-heeled shoes, and a book about sexual intercourse. That's how well the world in which I was born guarded the secret of sex.

*　　*　　*

I was contemptuous of that when I was young and cruel.
Now I am older and I think I understand what was going on.
It was how they protected us from being impregnated. They
didn't want that to happen to us. They didn't want us to
swell up with children and maybe die and begin the terrible
hard work of being mothers in a world where malaria flew in
the open screen doors or typhoid fever or yellow fever or
diphtheria or whooping cough or any of the terrible diseases
that filled the cemeteries while the land was being cleared
and the Mississippi Delta turned into farms, into a place
where people could live.

ᴄ₽

I USED TO GO to the coast every Easter, to a frame house on a
peninsula beside a bayou that becomes a bay that runs into
the Gulf of Mexico at the exact point where the state of
Alabama meets the state of Florida. There were seven houses
on our peninsula. With pine trees and white sand beaches.
The sun shone like diamonds on the blue water and in the
early mornings dolphins came into the bayou and swam past
the pier in pairs, rolling and touching, pushing and caressing
each other with their snouts.

During the summer months the houses would be filled
with my cousins, but the place was deserted at Easter and I
would go there to be alone and think things over at the point
where winter meets spring in my imagination. Well, not
really alone for I would have my children with me. But
almost never my husband, as I was usually "separated" from
him. I was young and confused during those years and I

would run home to my parents every time another child was born.

So it would be Easter and I would be alone on the coast. It is still cold there that time of year and I would lie in the sun covered with Bain de Soleil and goose bumps and read the *Four Quartets* out loud to myself while my wild redheaded children fought and built fires and collected firewood and drank Cokes and dyed eggs and wrote on themselves with ball-point pens and turned their backs the color of sunsets from bending over on the beach to build castles.

The *Four Quartets*. Thomas Stearns Eliot's great paean to the days of Easter. "Burnt Norton," "East Coker," "The Dry Salvages," "Little Gidding."

> *Home is where one starts from. As we grow older*
> *The world becomes stranger, the pattern more complicated . . .*

I would look up from my book, too young to know what all that meant. Too easily influenced to know there are other ways to grow old, that it can mean having the world grow simpler, clearer, more beautiful, less complicated. I would look down the beach. The children would be tearing into the sand with their shovels, launching their homemade kites, hauling up crab traps with their long, skinny, amazingly strong arms. They were all good swimmers. I never worried about them near the water. The real danger at Cotton Bayou was from the sun.

"You better get a shirt on," I would call out. "Or put on some suntan lotion. It won't be my fault if you get burned. Don't come crying to me when your skin falls off."

"As soon as we're finished," they would call back. "As soon as we get through."

"All right," I'd say. "I warned you. Don't say I didn't warn you." I would return to my book.

> *Time present and time past*
> *Are both perhaps present in time future,*

And time future contained in time past.
If all time is eternally present
All time is unredeemable.
What might have been is an abstraction . . .

"Momma," someone would cry out. "Marshall spit at me. Marshall and Garth said they're going to drown me."

"He got some wood from under the Johnstons' house," another voice would yell. "He stole the Johnstons' firewood."

"I did not. Besides, he stole my crabs. He let my crabs go."

"I did not!! Besides, the crabs belong to everybody. All the crabs are everyone's in the world."

"Momma said if I put out the crab traps the crabs were mind. *Didn't you, Momma. Didn't you say the crabs were mine!!*"

"Why don't you go in the house and get some Cokes," I would advise. "Get out the Hershey's and make some fudge for lunch. And leave me alone a minute, won't you. Can't you see I'm studying poetry?"

The concert would subside.

The Coke brigade would file past me up the stairs. I would return to Eliot.

Footfalls echo in the memory
Down the passage which we did not take
Towards the door we never opened . . .

Four Quartets. Maundy Thursday, Good Friday, Holy Saturday, Easter Sunday. The days slipped through my hands like music while the children's backs grew redder, the supply of Cokes smaller, the piles of wet clothes higher.

Sometimes other divorcées and their children went with us to the coast. The women and I would walk the lonely beaches talking about the men we had married and failed to love and stolen the lovely sunburned children from. We were full of brittle justifications. We could not figure out what had gone wrong. We had been so beautiful and gifted and polite. We had meant so well. There had been so much of everything. How could we be unhappy? How could we be alone?

The coast was a refuge for us during those hard years, a place of healing and reflection. We would walk the beaches together like women whose men have gone to war. Beside us the great pounding heart of the ocean, the sea breeze in our hair, the voices of our children rising and falling in the distance. We would walk the beaches and tell our stories until they assumed the qualities of myths. . . . "Momma," a child's voice would call out from behind a sand dune. . . . "I found a sandpiper's nest. . . . I found a cowrie shell. . . . I found a conch. . . . I found a red triton and Marshall says it's his. . . ."

℉

MY COUSIN Bubba Finley was a genius. He was the first boy in Issaquena County to build a radio that could talk to foreign countries. He talked to England and Australia and France and Mexico and the Caribbean islands.

Picture a two-story frame house beside a lake. There is a huge magnolia tree right in the middle of the front yard and screened-in porches around three sides. There is a parlor as big as a dance hall but no one ever goes into it except Bubba's twin sister, Laura. She goes in to practice the piano. Many rooms surround the parlor, going out in all directions, bedrooms, kitchens, halls. My aunt Roberta and cousin Nell are out in the yard practicing cheerleading in their heavy white wool sweaters. It is August and hot as the gates of hell but they have to wear them to get used to them for the fall. I want to be them more than anything in the world but I am

not. I am ten years old and I'm spending the week at Onnie
Maud's house as a reward for being reasonable about my
typhoid shot. Life is good.

It is midmorning, let us say, and Laura is in the parlor
playing *Clair de lune*. Across the road is Lake Washington,
the biggest cypress swamp in the world, mysterious and
beautiful in the morning sun. It is a lake left behind when
the Mississippi River changed its course and went to Greenville.

Onnie Maud's husband, Doctor Finley, is in his brick
office across the street giving shots and showing his skeleton
to children and telling ladies when their babies will come and
waiting for an emergency. At any moment a mule will step
on someone's foot or someone will break a bone or get bit by
a dog and have to have rabies shots or step on a rusty nail and
need a tetanus shot. I have seen them drag suffering victims
up onto Onnie Maud's porch right in the middle of Doctor
Finley's Sunday afternoon nap. The atmosphere hushed and
dangerous and afraid. He would rise from his bed. It seemed
as if he slept in his suit. He would take the victim into his
hands. No wonder his son turned into a mechanical genius.
Not that the radio was the only way Bubba's genius
manifested itself. He also had an unbelievable tenor voice
with a huge range. He would lie out in the backyard sunning
his lungs, then rise up and go about the halls, singing at the
top of his voice.

I adored him. I adored him more than his piano-playing
twin sister, or his wonderful older sister, Nell, or more than
Onnie Maud herself, with her unerring ability to make a
ten-year-old girl look like a princess by the application of a
curling iron and Laura Finley's beautiful hand-me-down
pinafores and dresses. Talk about genius! How those women
could sew.

The first time I made one of these broadcasts for National
Public Radio I thought of Bubba. I was in New York City

with earphones on my ears talking to Bob Edwards in Washington. A wonderful red-haired girl named Manoli Wetherall was in the control booth. There were soft white things on the walls reminiscent of the egg cartons Bubba used to line his room. I was enormously at home in that place. I felt as if I had been there before and I trusted it to be a place that was on a quest for truth, the only journey I am interested in going on. This is a writer's journal. You must understand how significant these relationships and correspondences seem to me. How I rely on them to tell me what to do next and where to go and who to trust in the world.

I RECEIVED a letter the other day from a woman in England. She loved my stories and sent me word that they made her want a mayonnaise sandwich and a Coke with a hole in the top of the cap. The letter was sent through my agent. It was part of a letter she wrote to him thanking him for sending her my books. She is the wife of one of his English authors but was raised in the American South.

"A mayonnaise sandwich and a Coke with a hole in the top?" my agent asked. "What is this strange southern meal? I have asked everyone in our office and even our resident Georgian cannot shed light on this menu."

Here is what I wrote in reply. *Dear Michael,* I wrote,

A long time ago people lived in houses where there was a constant supply of babies who drank out of baby bottles. I was fortunate to live in such a house and had baby bottles available to me anytime I wanted one so I never had to resort to the common practice of putting a hole in the cap of a Coca-Cola bottle with an icepick and sucking out the Coke.

I have, however, tasted this drink and it is indescribable, a combination of cola and cork and tin, and maybe even lead, dangerous and wild.

Part II. Mayonnaise sandwich. Take a loaf of white bread. Discard the ends. Eat a piece. Take two other pieces. Lay them flat on a plate. Open a jar of mayonnaise or Kraft Miracle Whip. Put as much mayonnaise as possible on each piece. Push the pieces together. Bon appetit.

Of such moments are the rewards of a writer's life concocted. The unfortunate part is that life imitates art so enthusiastically in my case at least that the minute I write down anything as seductive as the words *mayonnaise sandwich* I have to go and eat one. I always do it sooner or later — it might be days later — but what I generally do is go on and eat whatever it is right then and get it over with.

This is more than I need to know about the effect of thought upon action.

℞

I FOUND a note to myself on the back of a tablet this morning. Get back to that happy child lying in the yard in front of the house listening to China. That's what the note said. What it meant was, go back into the self, not the thousand masquer-

ades I am so adept at assuming. Back to that warm fat little
girl lying on the grass in front of my grandmother's house,
with the grass scratching my legs and the smell of the earth
and its incredible richness.

The bayou was going by not a hundred yards away but I
was not listening to the bayou. I was listening to China.
Right underneath me were thousands of Chinese people
hurrying through the streets of their crowded cities, carrying
marvelous paper umbrellas, pulling each other in carts,
endlessly polite and smiling.

Meanwhile, right there in Issaquena County, Mississippi,
I was in a house full of people who were also being very polite
to each other, on the surface, but underneath was China,
exciting undercurrents, alliances, power and usurpations of
power, statements and allegations and rumors. This was not
black against white or anything as mundane as that. No, this
was Onnie Maud in Glen Allen having allegedly made the
statement that Miss Teddy was grieving too long over her
dead husband and visiting his grave too often.

My great-grandmother, Babbie, and Eli Nailor, the cook,
were staying in the kitchen trying to keep out of it, but they
kept being drawn into the fray. I hung out in the kitchen all
I could in those days, as close as possible to the pantry where
they kept the pinch cakes, long trays of yellow cake that we
were allowed to break pieces off of in between meals, so I was
spending a lot of time on a stool by the pantry anyway and
got to hear everything that was going on.

There were German prisoners of war working the fields of
Hopedale Plantation that summer and there was fighting in
Europe and the Pacific and we heard reports of that every day
at noon on the radio. But the war that interested me was the
one that was raging between the big house and the house on
Lake Washington where Onnie Maud lived with her husband,
Uncle Robert, who was the only doctor for miles around.

Onnie Maud was supposed to have said that about Teddy

and a cousin in Rolling Fork had reported it and Teddy wanted to go up to Glen Allen and confront Onnie Maud and get it over with but my grandmother was against it and thought they should let sleeping dogs lie. The reason Miss Teddy's husband had died in the first place was because he was trying to save the levee, and she was only twenty-six years old at the time and pregnant and she thought she should get to grieve as long as she wanted to. Who was Onnie Maud to criticize her grief, up there in Glen Allen with her doctor husband in perfect health?

All that summer they would come into the kitchen one at a time and try to get my great-grandmother and Nailor to take sides but they wouldn't do it. Neither would I. I just kept on getting all the pinch cake I could and Nailor kept sitting on his chair saying this too shall pass away and my great-grandmother kept on making the mayonnaise. She would drop the Wesson Oil one drop at a time into the lemon and the egg, then beat it with the whip.

"What makes it mayonnaise?" I would ask.

"It's a colloid," she would answer. "Doctor Finley says it's a colloid."

I would stare off into the pantry, filled with the mystery of mayonnaise. Of course, this was a long time ago when people lived in houses where a lot was going on, and China was only the speed of dreams away.

⚚

I AM heavily under the influence this morning of a movie called *The Gods Must Be Crazy*, about a family of African bushmen in Botswana. These bushmen never say a cross word to their children and the children grow up to be the sweetest, gentlest, most lighthearted people in the world. Sir Laurens Van Der Post writes about these people, in books with wonderful names like *The Mantis Prayer*, and *The Lost World of the Kalihari* and *The Heart of the Hunter.*

I'm a sort of bushman. My mother never said a cross word to me. Even when she would pretend to discipline me, when she would knit her brows and screw up her lips and try to bring a little order into my life, I knew she didn't have her heart in it. I knew she thought it was funny as all get-out that I was wild and crazy. She still thinks it's funny.

She'd fit right in with those bushmen. She's got this gift of knowing that life is supposed to be a happy outrageous business. "Let's go shopping," that's her idea of how to discipline an unruly child. "I think you need some new shoes."

I almost never went to school. That's why I'm a writer. Anytime I wanted to I could wake up and say I was sick and she'd let me stay home and read books. If she came into my room I'd start turning the pages real slowly as if I was barely able to lift the book, or I'd clutch my stomach or my head. She would bring me cool drinks and bathe my face with a warm cloth and around noon she'd show up with a sickbed tray, chopped steak and mashed potatoes and baked apples dyed green, one of her specialties.

Then, when it was afternoon and too late to get sent back to school, I'd recover and get dressed and go outside and get in my treehouse and finish my book. I was reading about ten or twelve a week at that time. The stars on my reading chart fell off the board and dripped down onto the floor.

I really think this bushman stuff has a lot to do with my being a writer. I'm doing the same thing right this very minute that I did in the third grade. I'm all alone in a bedroom with some cookies and a drink, surrounded by books. When I get through for the day, when I recover, I'll get dressed and go down to town and see what's going on.

Why have I been doing this? What have I been trying to find out all these long years of my extended bushman childhood? What am I hoping to learn from all this character and scene and plot? I don't know. All I know for sure is that by this means, ever since I was a small child, every now and then I'd get a glimpse, like a shiver, of what's underneath the illusion, and it's the promise of another look at that that drives me to do this absurd thing for a living. An intimation of something wonderful and light, a chance to see what's really going on, stars and subatomic particles and so forth.

That's the thing that wakes me at dawn and keeps me in this room while everyone else is out in the real world making deals and talking on the phone and running the place.

We live at the level of our language. Whatever we can articulate we can imagine or understand or explore. All you have to do to educate a child is leave him alone and teach him to read. The rest is brainwashing.

♄

I HAVE BEEN moving around all my life. Going to different schools, living in different houses, shedding old roles, assuming new ones. This way of life is as natural to me as staying in one place is for other people. I do variations on the theme. I return to places where I used to be. I find my old personas. I try them on. If they still fit, I wear them out to a party or a show. If they begin to restrict my movements, I take them off. I am a human being, capable of mimicking anything I see or remember or can imagine. This week I am in the middle of moving back to Jackson, Mississippi. Finding my old friends. I am the hunter home from the hills, with stories to tell, news to catch up on, compliments to exchange.

I began my roaming life during the Second World War — every five or six months I moved to a new town and went to a new school. Some children are harmed by this process. I thrived on it. My parents are stable and enthusiastic people. A war had to be won and we were part of winning it. What had to be done would be done. I was raised to believe that people are brave and resourceful and resilient.

Now, here I am, so many years later, sitting in an empty apartment waiting for my furniture to arrive and I am perfectly happy and I have this wild idea that I know exactly what I'm doing and am in charge of my own destiny. I see myself as deliberately playing out an old scenario from my childhood. Tearing up a perfectly nice comfortable life and going off to live somewhere else. Deliberately complicating things.

Well, I am a writer and when life becomes comfortable for an artist the energy stops — nothing in the long history of our species has prepared us to be comfortable. Being comfortable is so boring it makes us drink and take drugs and bet on football games. Anything for a little excitement, so I invented this adventure for myself. My belongings are somewhere on a moving van between Fayetteville, Arkansas, and Jackson, Mississippi. My papers are scattered everywhere. My mind is like a pile of pick-up sticks, seeing new streets, new trees, new faces, learning my new address and phone number.

I wish I knew what I was really up to. A writer's mind is as full of tricks as a magician's. I might be running away from wondering if my new book is any good. I might wake up a year from now and decide this whole thing was either absolutely sane or absolutely crazy.

℞

MY GRANDCHILDREN are visiting me. Marshall Walker, age four, and Ellen Walker, age one — and I am watching the terrible pangs of sibling rivalry. This is real suffering and all I ever need to know about jealousy, its power and its source.

For a whole year Marshall has put up with this baby hanging on his mother and sucking on her breasts and sleeping in her arms. He has put up with her walking into his room and picking up his toys and getting all the attention.

But my house on the mountain is another thing. I am his grandmother. I belong to him, hook, line, and sinker. My piano belongs to him and my closet full of toys and my chairs and my pillows and my bed. Also, the box of huge wooden blocks a friend of mine always brings over when she knows he's coming.

Now this one-year-old baby girl is actually walking around this place touching anything she wants to touch. This is the first time she has been here since she could walk. He is going crazy. He sobbed himself to sleep the first night he was here, exhausted from trying to protect his territory. I am in such sympathy with him I have found myself taking sides against my own little granddaughter. These lessons are too hard to learn. This is more than I want to know about jealousy.

Be objective, I kept saying to myself. Then he would sit down to play the piano and here she would come, beating on the bass keys, ruining his music. Be objective, I warned myself. Then he began building a spaceship out of the blocks. He had been working for an hour stacking and arranging them, humming happily to himself as he formed the cockpit, the wings, the fuselage. She came walking out of the kitchen and destroyed half a wing with a sweep of her hand. He was on top of her in an instant. He grabbed her head in his hands. His mouth was open. I leaped over a stack of books. "Don't bite," I screamed. "Did he bite her?" his mother asked. "No," I said. "I stopped it. Come on," I added, grabbing him up. "Let's get out of here." We went out to the shed and found our old green tent and set it up under a maple tree and spread some sleeping bags on the ground and put the blocks on them and got a radio and put it in the window of the shed attached to fifty feet of extension cord and turned on KUAF's "Jazz and Fusion Hour." We have moved to the yard.

A psychiatrist friend suggests that the best thing to do is to show him the world is big and full of more exciting things than his mother's breasts. I agree. We're going to build telephones from the tent to the shed and start some swimming lessons and as soon as he gets home this afternoon I am going to call my older brother and apologize to him for being alive.

♆

THESE JOURNAL ENTRIES allow me to answer questions reporters ask me about my work. I am always dissatisfied with the reports that reach my readers. The boring little domestic details of my life don't seem to have anything to do with the mental life that makes the stories, with the real excitement of writing, the pitchblende I refine in search of radium. I'm so influenced by movies I saw as a child that that is actually how I view what I'm doing. I think of myself as a sort of literary Madame Curie in a shed in Paris surrounded by tables piled high with pitchblende. If I keep on trying, if I do the work,

I will find some light at the end. Remember the wonderful scene when she goes at night to her workshop, certain she has failed, and then sees the light shining from the petri dish? That's the sort of fantasy that leads me on.

I refuse to be cynical in any way about my work. My work helps me live my life. It tells me who I am. Take *The Annunciation,* for example — my so-called novel. What was that obsession with adoption about? I'm not adopted and I've never given a child away. Was it about my son in Alaska? When my middle son was eighteen, he handed me a high school diploma, got into a pickup truck, and drove up the Alaska highway to Fairbanks to work on the pipeline. He was happy as a lark, doing exactly what he wanted to do.

Meanwhile I was down in New Orleans, going crazy, staying up nights with outdoors catalogs, ordering triple-lined down coats and gloves and helmets guaranteed to work in the Antarctic and flare kits and sending them to him. I must have sent him half a dozen flare kits. Every day that child was in Alaska I would wake up and wonder if his eyeballs had frozen yet. He didn't even have a phone. I couldn't even call him up. It's not easy being a mother. It never ends. The child grows up and the mother keeps on mothering. It's pitiful. It drives you crazy. It drives you to write novels about adoption.

A critic once wrote to me and said, Ellen, for God's sake stop writing novels for therapy. It was good advice but how can I stop?

Anyway, my son didn't freeze to death in Alaska — he made a lot of money and spent it and learned how to take tractors apart and came home and got married and now he's farming in north Mississippi and I don't have to order any more flare kits or write any more books about lost children. Now I can go back to work writing about people who are looking for love in all the wrong places.

MY LITTLE redheaded grandchild has become very conscious of his hair. He fills the sink with water, then pulls a chair up to it, then very carefully, for he is a careful and precise child, he dips the top of his head down into the water. He looks in the mirror and smooths the sides down, then pushes up a small piece in the back.

"What have you done to your hair?" his mother said when she first noticed it. "It is the chicken look," he said. "I am the chicken style."

I suppose it was inevitable that sooner or later I must tell you about the overpowering joy of being a grandparent. People try to make light of this relationship. They say it is because a grandparent can give a child back to its parents when she becomes tired of caring for it. Not true.

His name is Marshall, this little boy that I adore. He has brown eyes and a wonderful large nose like Albert Einstein's and large ears like the Gautama Buddha's and I am sick at the thought that he must ever go to school. How awesome that one woman should have twenty or thirty children to care for all day. How could she help but make mistakes? Something is wrong at the very basis of our ideas about schools.

"The chicken look," he said. "I am the chicken style."

Last week I was down in Jackson, Mississippi, with my grandchild. I had taken him to visit my mother, that famous child-worshipper. We had Marshall, age three, and his cousin Heather, age four, and we had been at it with them for about twenty-four hours. I had them in the business of filling up a birdbath using eight-ounce plastic glasses. The birdbath is on the back of the yard in a bed of daffodils and the source of water is beside the house. About ten minutes of absolute peace had gone by. They were robotlike in their dedication to the idea of helping birds. I was feeling very powerful having hit upon this great idea to get them to leave me alone. I wanted to write about it. To describe the self-satisfied look on their faces as they filled the cups and carried them carefully back across the yard and dumped them in. What good citizens, helping the birds. I wanted to write about it but I didn't dare begin. I knew what would happen. The minute I got involved in my work they would sense I had stopped watching them and come running. I stood there thinking about what it would be like to be a young mother trying to write or paint or do anything alone in a house with small children. And yet life without them would be meaningless to me.

A poet told me that when her little boys were small she used to put her typewriter in the playpen and sit there and work while they tore up the house around her. Of course, she is an exceptionally energetic and resourceful person.

MY FOUR-YEAR-OLD GRANDSON and I were uninvited guests the other morning at the wedding of Sharon James to Jacob Clayton. It was a wedding in a castle. Along with my recent campaign to cure him of sibling rivalry, I have been taking Marshall out to explore the world. This being a Saturday we left early and stopped by the Station to pick up some muffins and then, carrying our boxes, we walked down to Wilson Park to eat breakfast in the castle.

The castle is a strange thing, rising up from the ground beside a creek that runs by the baseball diamond. It was built in 1979 by a sculptor named Frank Williams and was paid for by the National Endowment for the Arts. Frank employed CETA workers and at one time or another two dozen young people worked on the project, learning to mix concrete and lay stones and divert water, learning useful skills while they created magic.

The result is a real castle, built of stone and concrete, with a throne room and turrets and a bridge and towers that are inlaid with runes and small art objects and tiles bearing symbols both sacred and scary.

I had lunch at the castle on my forty-fifth birthday. But I had never been there for breakfast. Marshall and I arrived with our boxes and found the place packed with people wearing tuxedos. Sharon James and Jacob Clayton had hit upon the idea of getting married beside the moat.

There were bridesmaids in pink cotton, a bride in white lace who looked sixteen and not a day older. A three-tier wedding cake made by Josephine Banks, and a flower girl named Janie who emerged from her mother's car wearing pale pink and long gold ringlets. Marshall went crazy when he saw her and started flexing his muscles and making his motorcycle engine noise.

"I am never getting married," he said, when she had disappeared down the aisle beside the ring bearer. "I'm going to be an artist and paint and paint and paint."

Marshall is going through a difficult, highly critical, and generally unattractive phase right now. "Besides," he added, "it's going to rain."

I looked up. He was right. Rain clouds were gathering. Rain was on its way. But the preacher had begun the ceremony. He was already to the part about in sickness and in health and forsaking all others. The bride stared straight ahead. The maid of honor scratched her arm with a lace glove. I pulled Marshall's wonderful strong little body into my own and thought about the day his grandfather and I ran away to the hills of north Georgia to be married by a justice of the peace with a sheriff in attendance. We weren't much older than the children being married by this moat. Because of that this little boy exists and my middle age is charmed and rich and full of laughter.

"When are they going to eat the cake?" he asked, pretending to have lost interest in the flower girl.

"I was thinking of making some cakes this afternoon," I answered. "A pineapple upside-down cake and a marble cake and some cupcakes with colored icing. You want to help me do it?"

"Let's go," he said. "Let's go get started."

℞

I'VE BEEN UP in Chickasaw County, Mississippi, watching a house being moved down the Natchez Trace. My son, Garth Walker, and his wife, Jean Verrell, have taken it upon themselves to move a hundred-year-old house from downtown Houston, Mississippi, five miles out the Trace to Jeannie's farm. The weather has not been propitious for this undertaking. First there was rain, now there is snow. But my brave children are going right along with their plans. As of yesterday, half of the house (it had to be cut in two) had come to rest underneath a circle of oak trees and the other half will be moved today.

Jeannie's farm is on land that people in Chickasaw County call the Horsenation, a plateau where the Confederate Army hid its horses during the Civil War. Later, when the war was over, it was the site of many famous rodeos.

I watched the first half of the house being moved. I drove up the Trace and got to Houston just in time to see the house coming down the main street on a flatbed truck. Two men were standing on top moving power lines out of the way, and everyone in town had come out of their houses and stores to watch the progress.

Traffic was stopped for an hour in the middle of town, but no one seemed to mind. They have known Jeannie and her family a long time and if she wants to buy an old house and move it to her farm it's okay with them. Any tree branches that were in the way were cheerfully cut down and thrown to the side. This is rich and fertile land with many trees and no one minds losing a branch or two.

The house proceeded down the main street and turned onto Highway 389 and on down to the entrance to the Trace. My son was standing on the overpass with the park ranger. They were discussing the tendency of certain overprotective mothers to come driving up the Trace to make sure a house doesn't fall on anyone.

I watched the house move up the ramp and turn left onto the Trace. A chandelier in a bedroom swung gaily on its chain and I thought, Someday I'll be sleeping in one of those bedrooms holding a grandchild in my arms and I'll be telling him or her about the time I watched his house being moved along the Natchez Trace to his mother's farm.

I thought too of the Temple of Dendur in the Metropolitan Museum of Art in New York City, which was moved stone by stone from a little port on the Nile River to a glass-covered room on Fifth Avenue.

Man and his dreams, Stonehenge and the Great Wall of China and the Temple of Dendur and the Pyramids. The urge to civilization is to conquer or to build.

As I was trying to remember the rest of that quotation my son's house passed the Aberdeen exit and disappeared into the trees.

℉

IN THE LONG HOT SUMMERS of my so-called youth I used to put
on plays. I put them on in treehouses and on porches and in
basements. Basements were the best. In the first place they
were cool, in the second place they were mysterious, and in
the third place there was always a coal bin that the actors
could use for a dressing room.

The most memorable play I produced was in the basement
of a house in Harrisburg, Illinois. My co-director was
Cynthia Jane Hancock, who would grow up to become a head
cheerleader and drum majorette and, later, a finalist for Mrs.
Illinois. She was made for the stage. I, alas, was not.

This particular performance was a variety show. Cynthia,
dressed as Wonder Woman, would tap dance to "Meet Me in
Saint Louis." Dressed as Cat Woman, I would follow her
singing "The Desert Song." Our audience consisted of six or
seven neighborhood children and the son of the Harrisburg
newspaper editor. He was there with his camera, ready to
record for all time the premiere performance of *The Main
Street Review*.

It was ten o'clock on a Saturday morning in the very heart
of July. The audience was seated on a line of old footlockers.
The show began. Cynthia stepped up on the wooden stage
and wowed them with her rendition of "Meet Me in Saint
Louis." They screamed for more. She did "East Side, West
Side" and left the stage with a curtsy and a bow. It was my
turn. My Cat Woman costume was a green one-piece bathing
suit with a gold cummerbund and a black hat. I stepped up
on the stage. I opened my mouth to sing. It was my favorite
song. I had sung it a thousand times. Blue Heaven, I began.
Blue Heaven, Blue Heaven. What was next? I could not
remember. No words came. Blue Heaven, I began again. The
audience waited politely. They ate their popcorn and drank

their Cokes. I tried again. Blue Heaven. Blue Heaven and
You and I. Blue Heaven. The audience looked down at the
floor. I can't do it, I said. I can't remember the words.
Cynthia stood up. I guess the show is over, she said. You can
go home now if you want to.

℞

I HAVEN'T HAD a vacation from writing in ten years. Ever since
the afternoon in 1975 when I pulled my old portable
typewriter out of a closet and went off to the Caicos Islands
to write poetry, I've been writing or wishing I was writing
every single day from dawn to noon.

Now, suddenly, the spell is broken and I've been wildly
happy for three weeks — first I lost six pounds. Then I
bought some makeup. Then I decided to move back to
Mississippi into the bosom of my wild, beautiful family.

Don't get cocky and think you can go home again, a friend
warned me. Well, I'm going home anyway. If my father
wants to get up in the middle of the night and argue with me
about the Federal Reserve system, I'm ready.

If my grandchildren boss me around unceasingly, I'm
ready. If I have to fight for everything I've struggled to learn
and believe in, I'm ready.

Because I miss the state of Mississippi with its wonderful
fields and trees and rivers and bright-eyed imaginative
children.

Fayetteville, Arkansas, has been good to me. The quiet
beauty of the Ozark Mountains has given me the strength to
write three books of fiction and a book of poems and a play.

Now it's time to go home to the real material. To the place
where I was born and the beautiful musical language that I

first learned to speak. What you hear on the radio is only a ghost of those long vowel sounds. It is a language that's more like singing than like talking. So I'm going home. I'll fly back to Fayetteville and start packing up my papers and closing my little house on the mountain where I tried to be a slave to literature. That didn't work out for me.

I kept thinking about a poem by Louis Simpson called "The Springs of Gadera" about a man in publishing who dreams he is pushing a huge stone around a circle. One day he kicks his desk drawer shut and gets up and walks out. He looks back over his shoulder and imagines he sees some other poor guy pushing the same stone around the same old worn-out circular path. As for me, I'm tired of being a nun to art. I'm going to go live in the capital city of the state of Mississippi and find out what's going on in the modern world.

I CAN BARELY remember the Thanksgivings of my life. They fade into the late fall whiteness between Halloween and Christmas and there they lie, lost and forgotten or awash in a sea of rice and gravy and white meat. I never did like to eat dinner with large groups of people. I am more the type to take a sandwich up into a tree and nibble around the crust while I read.

The one Thanksgiving that I do remember was one in which I created something. At that time my parents lived on a farm in Rankin County, Mississippi, and my brothers and my three sons and my six nieces were there all the time anyway, so coming to Summerwood for Thanksgiving was nothing new. It was a wonderful creative time in my life. My parents were helping take care of my children. I was back in school at Millsaps College. Life was good. The children were still small enough to be manageable and I was writing and studying philosophy.

That Thanksgiving I decided to turn the day into a family Olympics. We marked off courses and had three-legged races and sprints and throwing contests and a steeplechase that consisted of a long course around the farm, over the dam, through the woods, around a barn, up and down hills, over a fence, and down a gravel road to a tent underneath an oak tree. I had been running quite a bit that fall and I am sure the driving motivation in my mind was that I would surprise and conquer my older brother, who once came in third in the real Junior Olympics. I have forgotten what came of that. I think he refused to race. Or else he raced but didn't try and infuriated me by letting me win. When we were small, one of my greatest complaints was that he let me win. "YOU LET ME WIN," I would scream, "YOU LET ME WIN. I HATE YOU." "Don't hate anyone," my mother would whisper.

Still, it was a wonderful day and we resolved to make the races an annual event. Two of my nieces were moved to write a newsletter about the day, which they copied on the office copying machine and sent around to the participants. That was so long ago. In 1967.

Recently one of the young editors found a copy and mailed it off to everyone who had been there for the first running of the Summerwood Thanksgiving Olympics. It was full of interesting interviews with the participants.

"My foot got hurt but I had fun anyway." Kathleen Gilchrist. "Tremendous success." Uncle Bob. I am quoted as saying, "Lovely healthy children are the greatest blessing of any year." And I might add from the perspective of 1986, especially when someone else is taking care of them most of the time.

ℂℙ

I KNOW SO MUCH MORE now than I knew then, except for a very long time ago, when I knew everything. I knew it all, where the barn was and how to ride the mules and where they kept the pound cake and how far to walk into the water without drowning, the smell of coffee and powder, the breasts of Babbie and Dan-Dan and Miss Teddy and Onnie Maud, the cold hands of Nailor. The soft bones of my mother, the bed of Aunt Roberta, how to get all the sugar I wanted, the way to Hannie's house and where the men had gone and why the women stopped what they were doing when the news came over the radio about the war.

Later, I would ride in the crop duster and be pulled on a board behind the motorboat and drive the new Buick around the pasture and wear slips that came from Memphis in boxes lined with pale pink tissue paper. I would grow up without noticing it since I had never thought that I was a child or seemed helpless or small to myself in any way.

I feared water unless they were with me and darkness and underneath the beds. I was afraid I would go rolling down the bayou bank in the car and forget to roll the windows up or down, whichever it was that saved your life. I was afraid I would be turned into a crow for lying, so I told the truth. Some of them regret teaching me that.

The black children came over in the morning to play with me. We played on the back porch and on the stairs behind the kitchen. We made doll furniture and chattered away in two languages. Their language was full of laughter. Mine was full of bossiness and warnings. I made the furniture and they admired it and ate the pound cake I got from the pantry and when it was gone they left. They wearied of watching me work so hard over nothing on such beautiful mornings with the ground so soft and fragrant beneath our feet. They would thank me very politely for the cake, then disappear. When they were gone I would put on my shoes and walk down the road searching for them. I would go to Ditty's house and ask her to find them for me. She would give me cornbread and let me watch her make spells. She was very good at making spells. She must have put a spell on me for me to be so lucky all my life. Yes, it must have been Ditty. For love of my mother she must have covered me with spells.

When we were away from Hopedale, sometimes for many months, I would write letters to them. Mrs. Stewart Floyd Alford, Hopedale Plantation, Grace, Mississippi.

In my imagination the mailman would drive his car down the gravel road from the Grace post office, past the Indian mounds and on past my godmother's house, past the shed where the crop dusters were parked and over the Hopedale Bridge and along the pasture where my grandfather's sheep grazed. He would stop the car and walk up onto the porch and hand the letter to my grandmother.

Dear Dan-Dan [the letter would say],

How are you? I am well. Danny died. He was run over and I stayed under the bed all day and would not come out. It is cold in Indiana but we like it here. Daddy has an A gas ration sticker and on Sundays we ride around in the car. We went to see some apple orchards and some goats. I will be there as soon as I can. Make some pound cakes and tell everyone I am coming. Your granddaughter, Ellen.

Dear Babbie,

Thanks for the letter with the good advice. I have read so many books there is no room for stars on my chart. I read about four a day and I am writing letters to everyone in Hollywood and everywhere we have been. We are rolling stones now, Daddy says. He says not to worry. Who wants to gather moss but mother wants to.

She says it drives her crazy to pack all the time. I don't care what happens as long as Dooley doesn't come in my room. He is spoiled rotten. They love him more than they love me, but you like me just as much, don't you? Granny doesn't like me at all compared to him. She only likes boys. Yours very truly, Your great-granddaughter, Ellen.

Dear Cousin Nell,

We are all so sorry your husband died. We cried and cried when the letter came. Please come and stay with us. You can sleep in my room. I hate to sleep there by myself. It won't help much but you have to do something. You can't stay in Glen Allen and grieve. I love you so much. You are my favorite person in the world. Yours most sincerely, Cousin Ellen.

I will do anything in the world to make you feel better. I have a new Jantzen bathing suit. It's two-piece.

Dear God,

I will never believe in you again for making Floyd die and Nell's husband and putting Dooley's eye out. You can count on this. I will never believe in you again because I didn't to begin with and I will spit on the floor if they make me go to church and kneel. I hate your guts. Who are you to make people die? I'm not going to. I'm going to be a vampire and live in the basement. If you are real strike me dead for writing this. See, you are a damn hell damn hell damn. Goddamn, Goddamn. It's going to be my favorite word. Yours very truly, Ellen Louise Gilchrist, September 1943.

Dear Diary,

This is the worst summer of my life. Floyd died and Dooley put out his eye and Momma is having a baby and we can't even go to Hopedale. The good part is the

46

war is about over and the lady next door gave me a dressing table with doors that swing in and out. I am going to cover it with movie star pictures as soon as I get time. There is a gold star on the door across the street and a gold star on Mrs. Mattingly's house and some of my teeth are coming out. I hope to have better news for you the next time I write. Yours very truly, Ellen Leigh. (I changed my name.)

Ellen Connell Biggs
Martin, Ellen Gilchrist's
great-great-grandmother,
for whom she is named

Margaret Connell
Biggs, maternal great-
grandmother

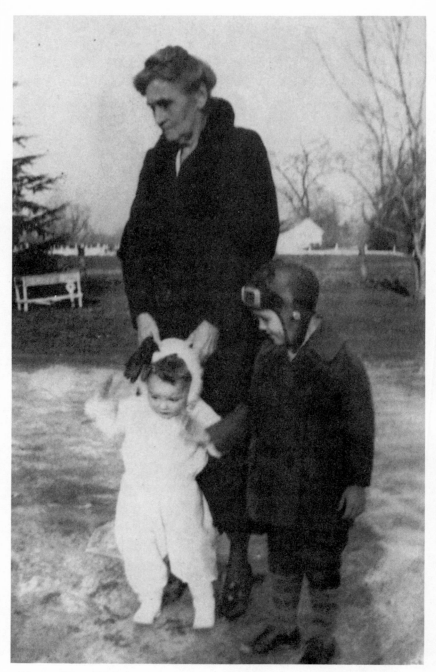

Young Ellen Gilchrist with great-grandmother Biggs and brother Dooley (William Garth Gilchrist III)

Paternal grandmother,
Louise Winchester Clark
Gilchrist, of Rosedale,
Mississippi, and Natchez

Paternal grandfather,
William Garth Gilchrist,
Senior, of Courtland,
Alabama

Nell Biggs Alford,
maternal grandmother

Stewart Floyd Alford,
maternal grandfather

Maternal grandmother and grandfather, Aunt Margaret on running board.
Great-grandmother holding mother in back seat, and Onnie Maud

Ellen Gilchrist's mother, "Bodie"
Alford, listed as "Most Popular Girl,"
Ole Miss, 1927

Mother at Hopedale
with Jiggs and Maggie

Mother at Ole Miss,
1928

Ellen Gilchrist's father,
pro-baseball infielder Garth
Gilchrist, known as "Dooley"

Father in 1979

Eli Nailor, baby Ellen, and dogs Old Joe and Bud

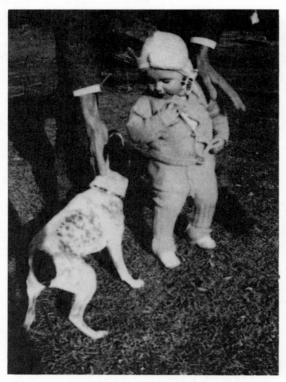

Ellen, Stewart Floyd Alford, Senior, her grandfather, and Jiggs

Dooley Gilchrist,
Roosevelt and Henrietta
Neal, and Ellen Gilchrist
on Steele's Bayou, fall of
1936 or 1937

Little Dooley, Eli Nailor,
little Ellen, 1936

Ellen, brother Dooley

Eli Nailor holding Dooley, George Healy IV (Bunky), Grandfather Alford, Roberta Alford, Roosevelt Neal, and Old Joe the dog

Jeanne Finney and Ellen (on right), 1939

Henrietta Neal, Nancy Crane, Ellen, Eli Nailor

Fourth of July parade, about eleven in the morning, Mound City, Illinois, 1939

Influences

I AM READING the correspondence of Gustave Flaubert and George Sand. I love these letters. They are a perfect match for me at this time in my life. George Sand was a settled grandmother of fifty-seven when she began this correspondence with a despairing Flaubert. She had given up her wild life and gone to live among her family in the French countryside near Nohant. She had a little granddaughter named Aurore whom she adored and she was deeply involved in the lives of her family and friends. She wrote movingly to Flaubert of their illnesses during the long French winters. There is a great charm about these letters. "A hundred times in life," she declares in one letter, "the good that one does seems to serve no immediate purpose: yet it maintains in one way or another the tradition of well wishing and well doing without which all would perish."

I was thinking of that this morning. I was out walking in my new neighborhood watching the early morning mist rising from these streets that were pasturelands when I left Jackson, Mississippi, eighteen years ago. Well wishing and well doing. How often I have tried to tell writing students that the first thing a writer must do is love the reader and wish the reader well. The writer must trust the reader to be at least as intelligent as he is. Only in such well wishing and trust, only when the writer feels he is writing a letter to a good friend, only then will the magic happen.

I have done the other thing. I have written bitter and cruel things and even published some of them and I regret them every one. This big brain of ours can think of anything. The job of the civilized man or woman is to choose what to keep and what to throw away. I want to love the world as George Sand did. I don't want the bitterness and despair of Flaubert.

His letters to her are full of sadness. He thinks the world is full of stupidity and cruelty and evil. George Sand also saw the evil of the world, but she did not think it was the ground of being. In a radiant passage she defends her utopian political ideals. "Everyone must be happy so that the happiness of a few will not be criminal or cursed by God."

Over and over in these letters Flaubert despairs, George Sand cheers him up and insists he must love the world. Their letters often cross in the mail.

I am sleeping well with this book by my side, feeling privileged to be allowed to share the record of this amazing friendship. The edition I am reading is the translation by Aimee McKenzie and it's hard to find. You will have to go to a library or have the book ordered by a bookstore. Most of the best reading in the world must be searched for in card catalogs or on dusty shelves in the back of stores.

♇

"A BODY does not experience itself as falling through space." Einstein called that the happiest thought of his life. It was the basis of the special theory of relativity and his search for a unified field theory.

A body does not experience itself as falling through space. This does not mean you or me falling from a ladder or the top of a ten-story building, although it can mean that too. It is Monday afternoon. I have been thinking about that concept since Saturday night. I had a debauch Saturday night. You all know what wild lives writers live. It began at four in the afternoon when I made the mistake of going to the bookstore. I left with three books, the New Modern Library edition of *On the Origin of Species* and *The Descent of Man* by Charles

Darwin, a book called *Darwin for Beginners* by Jonathan Howard, and the Abraham Pais biography of Einstein.

I was excited. I kept stopping on corners and reading. I went on up the mountain, ran into my house, stuck a diet dinner in the oven, and settled down on the couch to read.

I opened the Pais book on Einstein and began. "There was always about him a wonderful purity, at once childlike and profoundly stubborn. It is no art to be an idealist if one lives in cloud cuckoo land. He, however, was an idealist even though he lived on earth and knew its smell better than almost anyone else.

"Nothing was more alien to Einstein than to settle any issue by compromise, in his life or in his science. When he spoke on political problems he always steered toward their answer. Were I asked for a one-sentence biography of Einstein I would say he was the freest man I have ever known."

Oh, my God, I said. This will take the wide net. I turned off the diet dinner, picked up the phone, ordered a large combination pizza, and settled down — about nine thirty I could take no more. I went on off to bed. As always when I attempt to read about physics I am filled with wonder, a sense of ecstasy, pattern, texture, design. "Subtle is the Lord," Einstein said, "but he is not malicious." We are allowed to see what is going on. I went to bed without washing my face or hands. I snuggled deep down into the covers, for it is still winter here. I dreamed of fields of green going out from me in all directions. I was the center of the dream but not of the world. I fit into the plan of the world. I was in the right place and I could move. The fields stretched out — on and on — there was nothing frightening anywhere. Nothing that could not be seen and wondered at and understood. Nowhere I could not go by walking. I was not hungry or tired or scared. There were no snakes behind me in the grass, no insurmountable hills to climb, no unbridled horses coming to ride me down, no cars plummeting down hills toward water, no dragons to slay.

In the night I woke and opened all the windows so I could hear the wind blowing across the Ozarks. A body does not experience itself as falling through space. Because there is no fall and there is no space.

♈

I WILL BE fifty years old tomorrow. My fiftieth year to heaven, as Dylan Thomas once wrote. I read that very long poem out loud to myself every year on my birthday.

This year I am going to spend my birthday with the work of another genius. I don't know what genius is, but I know that when it breaks forth among us we recognize it and protect and cherish the gifts it leaves us. Bona fide geniuses are almost always very careless about leaving their work around in unprotected places. As if they know someone will take care of it for them. Or, perhaps, they can afford to be careless since they understand it springs from abundance, from an inexhaustible well.

All men honor genius, in all times, in all cultures, because it shows the rest of us what we can be, what we are made of, this dazzling, complicated creature we call man.

For my birthday, I am going to visit a house painted by a genius. The whole interior of the house is a mural of such brilliance and light that there is no way to describe its effect upon the mind of the viewer. Looking at that mural is like watching a child dance or a bird in flight. The mural was painted by Walter Inglis Anderson, who lived and worked in a place called Shearwater Pottery in Ocean Springs, Mississippi. Here, among his family and his children, protected from the world, he painted hundreds and hundreds of brilliant watercolors. He also carved huge wooden sculptures from fallen tree trunks and made murals and woodcuts and pottery and illustrations for children's books.

No one bothered him. No one told him to stop, or to do it another way. So he just got up every morning and did the work of a genius.

Often he threw a gunnysack full of canned goods into the bottom of a rowboat and rowed out into the Gulf of Mexico to a small deserted island that is part of the barrier reef that guards the Mississippi coast. There he painted everything that lives and breathes and moves. Hundreds of perfectly achieved watercolors on one and sometimes two sides of quite ordinary typewriter paper. When Hurricane Camille was on the way, he rowed out to the island and tied himself to a tree to ride out the storm protecting his island from the elements.

Genius is like a wild thumbprint. You can never look at trees or water or animals or yourself in quite the same way again after you have shared his vision. All he saw was magic and yet there is an orderly and logical intelligence to everything he wrote or painted. Pattern, texture, design, weave and weave and weave. "Wing, wind, wave. Wave, wind, wing."

He was in the habit of dashing off notes to himself on scraps of paper. On the backs of drawings or in the logs of his trips to Horn Island. Verses, aphorisms, stories, essays. An overwhelming mass of bits and pieces that fit together to reveal the shape of the quest he was on.

Here are some of the things he had to say.

"It is literally true that the demon to the student is technique. And it really is evil. Pay no attention to it, either in dancing or in painting."

"The evil to the beginning painter is confusion. Too many details. As he learns technique he forgets his demon and thinks he has defeated him with technique, but he has just given him a hiding place."

"True art consists of spreading wide the intervals so that the imagination may fill the spaces between the trees."

"The normal or even fairly normal man has to be almost knocked down physically to be anything but sublime. Why this is done I don't know. What reason is there against man realizing his sublimity I don't know."

"It is strange that the artist should have no standards and be constantly trying to live up to other people's standards."

"This is the supposition. I live and have my being in a world of space and forms which have color and shape. Consciousness of this means being alive."

"The first poetry is always written against the wind by sailors and farmers who sing with the wind in their teeth. The second poetry is written by scholars and wine drinkers who know a good thing when they see it. The third poetry is sometimes never written but when it is, it's by those who have brought nature and art together into one thing."

Tomorrow I will visit the house where the genius Walter Anderson slept while he was among us. As he wrote:

"If my ears were functioning properly I would hear, not just the wind in the grass, the two or three different rhythms of insects, the piping of a frog, the call of a nightjar, but an orderly and recognizable harmony, which might or might not have been written."

"A divine symphony. Wind, wave, wing . . . wing, wave, wind."

THIS IS part of a speech I wrote to celebrate Founder's Day at Scripps College in Claremont, California. I liked writing this speech because it gave me a chance to talk about something that is much on my mind right now. How wonderful men and women are and how long we have been wonderful. I wrote the speech four times. It ended up being more like a play in four acts than a speech. Here is Act Four.

I want to leave you with the idea that no theory is too wild to entertain for a while. You can entertain all the ideas you can think up or imagine. Later, in winter, you can decide which ones to keep and which to throw away. All of us are doing the same thing all the time anyway, all probing the same mystery, asking the same questions. Who am I? Where did I come from? What am I doing here? Is this right?

At the moment I have decided that for all practical purposes I can go on and assume that mankind, our species, *Homo sapiens sapiens,* is the only thing in the universe that is aware of itself. Our species, Man, on this beautiful watery planet, in this little piece of space and time, may be the only thing in the universe that ever was or ever will be aware of itself.

I have been reading a book by the scientist and philosopher René Dubos, called *Celebrations of Life.* Dr. Dubos writes about Neanderthal man, who was here on the earth one hundred thousand years ago. It used to be thought that these people were brutish and primitive, but they walked erect just like us and had brains as large or maybe larger. They had a full kit of tools, and, strangest of all, every fifth person in their bands has been identified as being over fifty years of age. This is amazing for a primitive hunting society.

Two of the old Neanderthal people found in the caves at Shandar in Iraq were so severely crippled that they must have been completely dependent on the members of their group for a long time. Also, these people buried their dead in graves lined with flowers. Clearly, we have been human for a long time. Clearly the first thing we did was probe the mystery and the last thing we will ever do is probe that same mystery.

I TAUGHT MYSELF to read poetry. Long before I could read prose I could piece together the words of nursery rhymes and poems. Long before I went to school I knew passages of Wordsworth by heart and the lyrics of many songs and would make up my own and write them down.

> *I am very happy now*
> *Dooley is dead and in his grave*
> *All his stuff belongs to me*
> *It's not my fault he drank poison tea*

Sometimes I would leave sibling rivalry as a subject for verse and branch out into metaphysics.

> *Oh, I love rain so much*
> *I love the skies and everything God made*
> *I hope he likes me too. If he doesn't, too bad for him*

I was mad at God. He had created a world full of bugs to bite me. Why did he make them? It made no sense to me. Later, when I was really angry with him about death, I thought back on his invention of bugs and knew that I had every right to be furious. If God made the world he wasn't good enough for me.

I think I knew early on that poets were as angry with God as I was. Certainly they were angry about death. Humpty Dumpty, what cynicism, what irony. All the King's horses and all the King's men. Thee and thou, the language of the Bible. A lot of sound and fury to cover up what God had done to us. I hated him. I sat up in a magnolia tree getting black from the bark and dared him to make me fall. I threw myself into rivers and dared him to make me forget how to swim. I filled my mouth with water and spat at the sun. Nothing happened. If he existed he was powerless. God reminded me too much of my father to be in good with me.

So poetry took the place of God. The wild cries of a thousand minds saying, Why did you do this, God? Who are you and why have you done this and since you did it, at least I'm going to call you on it. At least I'm going to make you stand up and face what you have done. My Last Duchess, the sphinx in the desert, oh, what are patterns for, Not one deserted dying, on whose forbidden ear, Go, Go, Go, human kind cannot bear very much reality.

On and on and on. Of course, there were also cries of lyricism and of love. I wandered lonely as a cloud, All I could see from where I stood, Oh, world, world, I cannot hold thee close enough. I also emitted great cries of praise, but not of God. It was man I was praising and the beauty of the earth.

Later, thinking over that poem about daffodils, I decided the main word in the poem was *lonely*. God makes us lonely and makes us die and the earth consoles us and gives suck, gives beauty beyond description and we go on another day.

How could men go into churches and praise the thing they call God? I asked myself. How could they praise something that has control over them, that rules them. What a bunch of bullshit. That's a poetic word I learned that came in handy when I was forced to sit in starched dresses and listen to preachers droning on in their sonorous and boring voices with that glazed look that comes over the faces of panderers and inveterate liars. I would squirm around on the seat. I would count the number of letters in the program, not counting punctuation marks; if the sum was an odd number, it meant Dick Lockwood loved me. If it was an even number, he did not. If it was an even number, I would do a recount including the punctuation marks. If it still came out even, I tore the program up and counted the words in a hymn.

That's what came next: after the panderer had put us all to sleep he would bring out a piece of music written by Bach and give God credit for that. The service would brighten up with the first chord of music from the organ. We would lift up our eyes unto the hills where the real world would hopefully still be going on when we got out of church. What was that all about? A poet knew.

> *ah Galexea Galexea*
> *to think it was your own little whim*
> *to invent him this man*
> *What was it?*
> *that you couldn't look with your own eyes*
> *at your armpit?*
> *you couldn't see your own beautiful back*
> *graceful as a beach*
> *and you wanted someone to walk*
> *its lovely loneliness a while?*
> *a while only?*

That is part of a long poem by Alvaro Cordona-Hine, and I have kept it with me for years and read it to thousands of people and once read it on National Public Radio and once read it late at night to a room full of people at a Book and Author dinner who probably had something else in mind besides hearing me read a long philosophical poem by a real writer. I read the poem and then I got up and left so I wouldn't have to hear the speeches made by the romance novel writer and the country-and-western writer wearing the hat and smoking the big cigar while we ate dinner. After that night my publisher decided it would be best to keep me home and sell the books the best they could without me.

But I was talking about poetry. There weren't any poets at the Book and Author dinner. There aren't many poets anywhere anymore because the poetry isn't lyrical or much good or memorable and besides no one wants to read it but the same bunch of teacher-poets who write it and they are too cornered to allow anything wonderful to happen in poetry. If a good poet begins to raise his or her voice, they kill him with criticism. "Lyrical wheel-spinning," that's the kind of thing they say to young poets who are letting their hearts sing. So no one loves poetry anymore and no one wants to publish it and no one wants to buy it and all of that has taken the heart out of young poets. If a young poet showed up today with a poem that began, "It was my thirtieth year to heaven," he would be laughed off the block.

Here are some of the poets it is no longer fashionable to emulate. Edna St. Vincent Millay, who at nineteen could write, "All I could see from where I stood / Was three long mountains and a wood; / I turned and looked another way, / And saw three islands in a bay. . . . Over these things I could not see; / These were the things that bounded me."

Anne Sexton is another poet the Academy would like to forget if possible or at least send to the back of the class. Anthologies never do her work justice and she is being passed over as a subject for serious study. Still, while she was writing she spoke to us with a voice as real and lyrical as the sea and my generation of women learned about ourselves from her. "I am torn in two but I will conquer myself," she wrote. "I will take scissors and cut out the beggar. I will take a crowbar and pry out the broken pieces of God in me."

"The sea is very old," she wrote. "The sea is the face of Mary, / without miracles or rage / or unusual hope." And

> I am surprised to see
> that the ocean is still going on.
> Now I am going back
> and I have ripped my hand
> from your hand as I said I would
> and I have made it this far
> as I said I would
> and I am on the top deck now
> holding my wallet, my cigarettes
> and my car keys
> at 2 o'clock on a Tuesday
> in August of 1960.

How I love the wild lyrical language of the poets. I knew a poet once and spent many days and nights with him and took walks with him and went into shops with him and watched the world with him and learned to adore the beauty of the world and despise its sadness. I must write of him someday and tell the world what it was like to know a great poet and be his friend. When he killed himself over some long-buried sadness, I could not bear to remember him and threw away all his books and all his letters and everything that had anything to do with him except an unpublished manuscript that was dedicated to me. It's still around. Even in my sadness and rage I couldn't throw that away.

What else? The Arabs believe there are three causes for celebration. The birth of a son, the foaling of a stallion, and the emergence of a poet. One is emerging somewhere now who will write the poem that will solace and teach me in my old age. I raise a glass to that poet and dedicate my song to him.

FIFTEEN YEARS AGO I bought my first real painting. I remember the strange quality of that week, while the painting sat in my living room, and while I pondered the possibility of actually spending *three hundred and fifty dollars* for something to hang on a wall.

On the side of buying the painting was a line I had read somewhere by Gertrude Stein. She had said you can either have great paintings or you can have great clothes, and that she had chosen to have paintings. Also, I kept remembering once when I was nineteen years old and was in Birmingham, Alabama, with fifty dollars to spend. It was a bright January day at the end of Christmas vacation and I was standing on a sidewalk halfway in between a clothing store, where a pair of gold cocktail shoes with three-inch heels was begging me to buy them, and an antique store, where an old handmade cobbler's bench was on sale for exactly the cost of the shoes. I kept going back into the antique store and marveling at the patina on the wood of the bench, sitting on it, as a real cobbler once sat, and rubbing my hands along the smooth dark sides.

In the end I went into the clothing store and bought the tight uncomfortable golden shoes and left the bench. I had cast my lot with vanity and I knew it. That bench haunted me for years. Every time I wanted a table to go beside a sofa or a place for a child to sit and color I would think about the wide purpose of the bench, the intelligence of its design.

Meanwhile the golden shoes had carried me to a lot of drunken fraternity parties and disappeared into the destiny of cocktail clothes.

Now, some years later, I walked in and out of my living room past the beautiful painting that I was trying to make up my mind to buy. It was the first work I had seen by the American realist Ginny Crouch Stanford, who later would become my friend and paint the brilliant paintings which would become my book covers, and the story of that damn cobbler's bench kept pounding in my head, a moral tale if there ever was one.

Finally I gave in. I wrote a check and mailed it off and the painting was mine. I think I should note that I was properly appalled that I could so easily become the proprietor of another person's work and ran out and wrote a will leaving the painting to the painter at my death.

It is still my favorite painting. It keeps getting closer to me. It hung for many years above a fireplace. Then above a baby grand piano. Now it is beside my bed, on a wall that looks out upon a lake. "Those eyes," people say when they look at it, meaning the beautiful, haunting face of the young black-haired girl who leans in the painting against a marble statue of an angel. "My God, those eyes."

"I know," I answer. How long that painted look has lasted and never lost its power to charm and amaze.

Once I made that initial plunge into buying art, the rest was easy. I didn't buy another pair of high-heeled shoes for years. I didn't buy cocktail clothes or new placemats or recover the sofa. My money was spent on paintings and pieces of sculpture and pottery and photographs. By the time I left New Orleans and went to live in a simple light-filled house in the Ozark Mountains, the only things I cared enough about to pack up and take with me were these beautiful individual products of other minds and hands. For seven years I lived alone in a small frame house on a mountain and hardly ever bothered to lock the door. Anybody that wanted to steal the things in that house would have been someone I wanted to meet. I don't think I ever lost sight of how fortunate I was to spend my days and nights surrounded by the best moments of some of the best minds of my culture.

Finally, I had accumulated too much wonder. I was in danger of becoming a museum curator, which is a fine occupation but not a good thing for a writer, who needs to travel light and stay flexible.

So I have gone into phase two of my fascination with art. I have started giving it away. I am fortunate in having three sons who also love beautiful things, and among them I am able to keep many walls and flat surfaces covered with art in various cities in the southeastern part of the United States. I lend them paintings and photographs and they lend them back to me. I will turn a corner in one of my children's houses and there is a painting I bought one snowy January day in Boulder, Colorado, or, I'll enter a room in an apartment and there is a piece of pottery from the day I discovered the famous Calabash potters of Fayetteville, Arkansas.

Life will not give us everything we want. It will not give us happiness, or "the seven Visigoth crowns in the Cluny Museum," as Elinor Wylie once wrote. But it may give us "a very small purse, made of a mouse's hide. Put it in your pocket and never look inside."

Art civilizes and makes clear. Living with art is charming, in the old sense of the word. The art object draws you into it, does a little dance for you, calls up, praises, sings. God Love Artists, my daughter-in-law once wrote to me on a postcard from the Museum of Modern Art's exhibit of Picasso. They Make It Right.

♈

THE NEW ORLEANS PHOTOGRAPHER Clarence Laughlin was a friend of mine. He was a genius. Genius can not be dissected or understood. It can only be loved and celebrated and wondered at.

Clarence was a New Orleanian and proud of that fact, but in his heart I think he was always a child of the bayou country. He drank its sugary wines and honored its legends until his death this January at eighty. He gave up its sugary tongue, however, and taught himself to speak in such a way that almost no trace of his Cajun accent remained. More about this later. First I want to talk about his magic.

Everything about Clarence was magical. In his presence you could believe in magic or destiny or kismet. He thought it was kismet that we came to know each other. He felt this way about many of his friends.

I had heard of Clarence. One day another photographer came tearing into the offices of *The Courier,* where we both worked, showing us photographs and copy for a story about Clarence. "You won't believe this man," he was saying, or words to that effect. "He's incredible. He knows everything."

I looked at the photographs. There was this smooth-cheeked white-haired man with piercing eyes already demanding something from me. Some answer. Some return. There were also pages of quotations. I read them with great interest and attention.

About a month later a friend took me, on a cold rainy Sunday afternoon, down to the Faubourg-Marigny to see an exhibition of Clarence's work and hear him speak. It was a new gallery with tall freshly painted walls and high ceilings. People were milling around drinking wine and talking in quiet voices. There was violin music on the stereo. And on the walls were the most incredible photographs I had ever seen. Absolutely original, as was their maker. He came into the gallery, wearing a coat thrown over his shoulder like a cape, and took the podium and began to talk about art in a way I had never heard. About the relationship between art and the subconscious mind, about the forms art takes in its insistence on telling us what we're thinking. About how art takes us past the veils of illusion and returns us to ourselves. About what a photograph means and why light and shadow fascinate us, about how unique we are and how alike, how mysterious we are and how predictable. I was dazzled.

I ordered two photographs and went home and wrote him a long letter in answer to the questions he had raised in my mind. Later, when I knew Clarence well and became his friend, I would drive him to the Lafayette Station post office to pick up his mail, boxes of fan mail from all over the world. I suppose when I wrote him I thought I was the only one who did.

Anyway, I mailed off the letter, not expecting or even particularly wanting a reply, and in a few days he called me. There was his rough, exciting, enormously civilized voice on the phone, inviting me down to the Pontalba to see his books.

At that time he had a huge apartment in the Pontalba overlooking Jackson Square. It contained a library of almost two hundred thousand volumes. They were the most incredible books I had ever seen. Clarence slept on a small bed in the midst of those bookshelves. He could put his finger on any book without consulting a catalog. But then, he only got out the ones he was interested in. You could ask all night but he would not produce a book he didn't want to talk about.

As soon as I arrived that first night we went right to work. Clarence got out some books and began my education. "Look," he would say, "look at this. You must understand this. Listen to what I'm telling you." Leonor Fini, the French surrealist poets, Balthus, Klimt, Lafcadio Hearn, British illustrators, Italian cartoonists, the lists of things I must learn and "be exposed to" went on and on.

Oil interests in the gulf, people destroying the wetlands, plastic cups, undisciplined children, women smokers, unlettered so-called writers, Mayor Moon's attempts to bring a sound and light show into Jackson Square, the list of things he hated and warred against was also long.

"But, Clarence," I would say finally, "I want to see your photographs. I came to see your photographs. Please show them to me." Then, grumbling, he would get out a stack of prints and begin to tell me how they were created. Created they were. Planned and executed with the care an architect takes with a building. Only Clarence was the planner *and* the builder *and* the carpenter and the plumber and the one that cut the trees down to get the lumber.

It wasn't easy being his friend. You had to be able to move fast. Clarence was full of ideas and he feared nothing except having his knee give out or his books cut up by greedy dealers. He was haunted by the idea that someone would get hold of his treasured art books and cut them up and sell the pages.

At the height of my friendship with Clarence he had me in a car one spring day driving down to Terrebone Parish with four surrealists from Chicago in the back seat. We were going to see the cemeteries. I was driving my small blue Datsun. The surrealists were huddled together in the back seat. Clarence was riding shotgun, telling me how to drive and reading the map and lecturing about Cajun cults of death and black silk funeral flowers and enamel photographs of the dead and carvings on tombstones and surrealism in general and the bad state of the arts.

He turned to me suddenly, as if he had just remembered something important. "I've been meaning to tell you that whenever you have time we can start our diction lessons," he said.

"What?" I answered, for this was new to me.

"I've decided to teach you to speak properly," he said. "So that people will take you seriously." The surrealists looked down at their hands, embarrassed for me.

"That's okay," I said. "I'll just stay like I am."

"Of course not," he said, and went back to the map. "It took me a long time to learn to speak correctly but I learned. You will learn too." Alas, we never had time for our lessons.

I learned of his death by reading of it in *Time* magazine. It was a cold wet winter evening. I was at a newsstand on the corner of Third Avenue and 73rd Street in New York City. I bought the magazine and stuck it in my pocket and walked outside and stood on the street thinking about the last time I had seen him, the night he showed me his new darkroom in the library he built onto the back of his wife Elizabeth's house in Gentilly. Then I thought about the last month he spent in the Pontalba, about how bad his knee had become and how he cursed it. About the hundreds of boxes of books he had packed and the pulley system and cardboard chute he invented to lower the boxes down the three flights of narrow rickety Pontalba stairs. I thought about the expression on our faces as Clarence outlined his plan to sail the boxes down from floor to floor.

That night I had a dream. In the morning I began to develop it into one of my Journal Entries for National Public Radio. The dream appeared to be about Picasso but as I developed it I saw it was really about Clarence. In such a way the mind gives up its secrets. I call it magic. Clarence called it art. Here then is the dream and its unfolding.

Journal entry, January 18, 1985,
New York City, New York

I dreamed last night of Picasso. We were driving through the Delta looking for a house for him to use as a studio. We were in my little blue Toyota. I was driving. Picasso was in the jump seat. "They gave me everything I wanted," Picasso said. "Money and fame and beautiful lovers."

"They let you paint your chairs," I said. "That was the good part."

"I painted what they wanted," he said. "The more ridiculous it was the more they liked it."

"You were a genius at fourteen," I said. "What else could you do? You had to find ways to make it more amusing."

"I needed blue," he said. "I wanted a blue made of ground-up sapphires. If I had had the right blue. It really made me mad not to find that blue."

"You did all right," I said. "You did just fine."

"*Guernica,*" he said. "They all wanted *Guernica.* Look at the drawings, I told them. Look at the eyes on the women. Look at the love scenes. *Guernica,* they demanded. Show us war."

"It was wild," I said and we laughed together at that. Two artists out for a drive in the country. It was a bright spring day in the Delta. The sun made mirages on the asphalt road.

"I was always afraid of running out of water in the desert," Picasso said. "I was afraid I would end up chasing mirages."

"That's deep," I said. "That's very deep."

"I know," he said and settled down into the jump seat. "But who can bear to live on the surface?"

In real life I also hang out with painters and potters and photographers. They are the best friends a writer has. They teach you to use your eyes.

Clarence Laughlin was my first artist friend after I started writing, a wonderful, outlandish, completely original man. He gave me the cover for my first book of poems. Just gave it to me. A beautiful photograph of a Welsh actress. One night Clarence came to my house to take me to a double feature art film. *Siddhartha* and *Steppenwolf*. My husband came home as Clarence and I were leaving and asked politely if I would make him a sandwich before I left. Clarence hit the ceiling. We are going to see art, he said, drawing himself up on his walking stick. You can eat anytime.

My husband apologized, grabbed a piece of cold bread, and the three of us rushed off to the movies.

♈

I WAS OUT WALKING on the mountain with a friend named Kathy last week. She had just returned from a visit to Seattle, and was full of descriptions of the mountains and the forests and the wildflowers. She told me she had run into an old friend named Greg who said he was driving to work one day last February and heard me say on the radio that we should all learn from two-year-olds and go to work by different routes and take all our books off the shelves and throw them on the floor and play with them.

So that afternoon he went out and bought a red motorcycle and named it for me and now he goes to work in a different way.

"Oh, no," I said to Kathy. "I'm scared to death of motorcycles."

"Don't worry," she said. "He's a responsible person. He'll be careful and not get hurt."

It was the first cool day. We walked awhile in silence. I kept thinking about all the ruts I've let myself get into lately and how I can talk a good game but where is the action and so forth. Kathy turned off on Spring Street and I walked on home and went into my house and started pulling all the books off my bookshelves and piling them up on the living-room floor. Pretty soon I had a carpet of books. It looked great. I found a set of charcoals behind the books and drew a picture of myself and then one of a tree and then I found an old Japanese fan I bought years ago in New Orleans. Then I sat down to read. I found Loren Eiseley's *The Star Thrower* and my book of Karsh's photographs and I marveled over the photographs of Tennessee Williams and the mystical one of Martin Luther King.

I am here to report that my advice about taking down those books was sound. Not only was it a good idea but it was the beginning of one of the best weekends I've ever had. I picked up Judy Dater's book of photographs with the wonderful cover photograph of Imogen Cunningham standing by a tree in her long black dress with her camera strap embroidered with peace signs and went downtown to show it to someone. I wandered into the Restaurant on the Corner and found the jazz pianist, Leland Tamboulian, and he wanted to see the books so he came up and played the piano while the sun went down and some more people came over and someone found *The Rubáiyát* of Omar Khayyám and had to read it out loud and one thing led to another and the whole weekend was infused with a wonderful sense of fun and good humor all thanks to Greg Simon of Seattle, Washington, who reminded me of something I must have known for a while in February but had forgotten in the dog days of August.

Work

*H*OLLYWOOD AND the writer: so the first thing that happened was I had this successful book of short stories called *In the Land of Dreamy Dreams*. That same year the twenty-five-year-old daughter of a friend in Jackson, Mississippi, won a Pulitzer Prize for a play. She was out in Hollywood turning down offers as fast as she could answer the phone, so she told one of the producers at Twentieth Century Fox to call and offer one of the deals to me. Deals, that's what they call them out there. It reminds me of my brother and me matching nickels with our lunch money in the sixth grade.

I was in my kitchen in Fayetteville, Arkansas, one afternoon in 1980 and the phone rang. It was a businesslike voice calling from Hollywood and offering to give me sixty-five thousand dollars to rewrite the Italian film *Wife-mistress* and set it in New Orleans. You've got to be kidding, I said. Why on earth would you want to do something like that?

That was before I knew you are supposed to say, Oh, yes, what a marvelous idea. How did you ever think up something so wonderful? That is the proper response to a Hollywood producer. Oh, my, what a wonderful brilliant idea. Gee, I'm honored you called me in on that. Besides, I didn't know anything about publishing or movies at the time and I thought sixty-five thousand dollars must be some magic number of dollars they gave away right and left. I had just been offered almost exactly that amount of money for something else someone thought up for me to do. I didn't know yet that all you got to begin with — up front, they call it — was a very small amount of money and you had to work for months or years even and then it was highly unlikely that they would ever give you the rest of the money. Also they make you feel like it's you who has failed, never that it was they that couldn't pull the deal off — Hollywood is really as sleazy as it's reported to be. It chews up writers and spits them out. It wastes their time and their dreams.

I didn't know any of this yet. "Well, listen," I told this producer, trying to make her feel better about coming up with such a dumb idea, "I've got a lot better ideas than that for making movies." Oh, she said, tell me. So I told her the entire plots of about three movies and even called her back on my own money to finish one I had to interrupt to go to the door. So she wrote that all down and I never heard from her again.

I found all of that very interesting. Later I had some more offers of about the same kind — I just kept turning them down. I am saving myself for something I can believe in — that's how crazy I am.

℞

UNIVERSITIES are always after me to give them my papers (by which they mean my letters and notes and worksheets). Whenever that happens I go out to the shed and get a sack of them and burn them up in the wood stove. I hate the idea of some poor graduate student down in a marble basement somewhere going through my notes and letters and wild imaginings. These pieces of paper are meaningful to me because any time I look at one of them it reminds me of what I was doing when I wrote it. But why should some stranger waste his time on my worksheets?

A poet told me a good one the other day. She said academics have a new name for a writer's worksheets. They call them repressed papers. Here are some of my repressed papers. I found this notebook on the floor by the piano this morning. It's been there for months.

To comprehend the major blueprints. An event occurs in three dimensions of space and one of time, or motion?

A four dimensional space time continuum. Is time motion? Yes, it seems so.
The simpler the premises the wider the area of applicability.
The heuristic view that light can be both wave and particle.
The questioning of causality. Always we have taken for granted the idea that every event could be explained by its antecedent conditions.

What is random?
DO THE LAWS OF CAUSE AND EFFECT GIVE WAY TO THE LAWS OF CHANCE AT THE ATOMIC LEVEL?
The equivalence of all inertial systems in regard to light.
Inertia. The tendency of a body to resist acceleration.
Light is composed of discrete packets or quanta which move without subdividing and which are absorbed and emitted only as units.
Light is composed of quanta.
The study of the very small is quantum physics and the study of the vast realms of space is relativity.

I will name the new book *Light Can Be Both Wave and Particle*. In memory of *Everything That Rises Must Converge*. Remember how that title haunted me and how hard I tried to know what it meant? Yes, *Light Can Be Both Wave and Particle*.

* * *

"Wave and particle?" my editor said and shook his head. "Why not, it suits me if it suits you."

℞

MORE REPRESSED PAPERS:

> I would still be a writer whether or not I had ever been
> in psychoanalysis but I would be a different writer,
> more driven, frightened, wild and unsure, a poet hiding
> behind the mask of poetry, talking in riddles,
> obsessed for days with words like riddles,
> caught in traps of language,
> unable to understand the sources of language or my own
> subconscious motivations and drives.
> I would not know as much, maybe.
> Maybe I found out as much writing as I did talking.

Psychoanalysis is the impossible profession. The terrible paradox is that the knowledge gained by psychoanalysis is not of much use in the real world. No, that's not true. It's of use to a writer. The terrible problem is that the knowledge is not transferable.

My Freudian said I was not in analysis. I would never lie down on the couch. I sat cross-legged on the floor looking at his shoes. He would never let me touch his shoes. Anyway, I think I am funnier and wiser and more balanced because of it. I like myself more and trust myself more. Of course, I might have been that way because I got older. Or maybe it's just because I've gotten up every day for eight years and done my work and am still doing it. Maybe my work healed me of the small amount of civilizing I was exposed to. Guilt is too high a price to pay for civilization. There's got to be a better way.

I was sitting on a bed in a New York apartment arguing with my cousin about God.

"Who made you?" she demanded.

"I don't know."

"You think you're so powerful you made yourself?"

"I didn't say that, Baby Gwen, you said that, don't put words in my mouth."

"Then what do you believe? Even you have to believe in something."

"I believe that man takes his own goodness and sets that intelligence outside of himself and calls it God and worships it. And then he takes his natural ability to transmit thoughts and he calls that the power of prayer. It's all semantics. It's all words."

"You have to make the leap of faith. Someday you'll do it."

"I will not."

"It's all faith. It's faith and grace."

"It's twelve o'clock, Baby Gwen, and we've been arguing this for thirty-seven years. I'm going home."

We get up from our mutual great-great-grandfather's bed which my cousin keeps in an apartment in New York. We hug and kiss and go our separate ways.

I walk out into the streets of New York City at night. Lights that man invented and made out of his greatness are all over the place on the streets and above. Through a crack in the skyscrapers are other lights, wildly, crazily dependable somehow or other in case it is true that the earth is round and moving on its axis among the stars.

℄

I KNOW a lot of two-year-olds that have genius. They are terribly observant, absolutely curious, willing to take risks. They will pay endless attention to detail, will return over and over again to a problem until it's solved. Suddenly, they make the final move, the cap is off the bottle, the cabinet is open, the door is unlatched. My children were escape artists. They ran away to have adventures. I have chased them through the streets a million times, in my nightgown or in the rain. The oldest one was the best at it. When I found him he would be sitting in some stranger's house eating cookies. He knew how to pick his victims. They would usually be people about the age I am now. Do you remember how marvelous a stranger's house smelled when you were small? That's another mark of genius, the senses are keen and finely tuned.

How to hold on to that native genius and also learn the things we need to know to survive. How to hold on to the breadth of genius and still narrow it down enough to concentrate on one piece of work. How not to allow the narrowing to become more important than the whole. These are big problems. I'm thinking about them all the time. How not to let the world de-genius us, our children and our grandchildren and our friends.

Here's one thing I know for sure — you have to stay flexible. You have to have a lot of possible moves so no one can get you in a position where you think there's only one way to live or only one way to solve a problem. A Jungian I know used to make me so mad telling me a story over and over about a friend of his who refuses to eat in the same restaurant twice or drive the same route to work in the morning. Oh, I know, I would say when he told me that story. You've already told me that, don't tell me that again.

No, he would answer, hear me, you aren't listening. Then he would tell it to me again. It was a long time before I began to see the wisdom of that story. Every time I would do something like take a different path when I walked downtown, I would say, Oh, my God, this is so silly.

It is silly. That's the point. It's divine and silly. It's the stuff that genius lives on. To constantly sample the riches and variety of life. Watch a child move from one activity to the other, moving around a house, never exhausting the possibilities of any one thing before moving on to the next one. We say of children, they are into everything. We should be into everything. We should get up one morning and take all our books and put them in a pile in the middle of the floor and start playing with them. Euripides and Aeschylus and Hemingway and Thornton Wilder and Margaret Mead. Faulkner and Edna Millay, and oh, yes, *The Conquest of Mexico* and *The Conquest of Peru* which I borrowed years ago from my ex-husband. Maybe I'll mail them back to him for his birthday.

I AM GEARING UP to go to New York for two weeks to oversee a professional reading of my play. It is a play that I began in New York in February of 1984. I began writing it during the first act of Sam Shepard's *Fool for Love*. I wrote all over my program and my agent's program. Then I went home through a blinding New York rainstorm and wrote all night in a hotel room. The next day I had lunch with my agent and told him I'd been up all night writing a play.

I told him the story, then I put the play away for three months. In June I had to go to Lincoln, Nebraska, to teach for a few weeks so I took the notes with me and there, in a basement apartment near the campus, I hammered out three full acts in less than a week and sent it to a typist.

Since that time the play has undergone four major revisions, elaborating and extending what is there, taking stuff out of the stage directions, which at one time contained a lot of the best material, and putting it back into the play. I am, after all, a fiction writer not a playwright and had to transpose the work from one form to the other.

Now, the American Place Theatre is going to have a professional reading of the play with a fine actress playing the lead. I'm excited and scared, but the day I no longer do anything that frightens me and makes me shy I will know I am finished as a writer. And of course I'm hoping that around eleven o'clock one night they will say, "Oh, Ellen, you have to rewrite the second act," and I'll say, "Don't worry, I'll do it tonight," and so forth. I'll emerge from a hotel room the next morning holding a brilliant revision and everyone will cheer. I keep thinking about a passage from a book by Georges Simenon.

"Why do we read?" he asks, "why do we go to a show? Imagine an entomologist, an observer of insect life, suddenly witnessing the exodus of a quarter of the inhabitants of an anthill, at a time of day when they normally would be sleeping. They are going off to a mysterious appointment. He sees them jostling each other and converging towards a clearing where the soil rises in tiers. In order to enter that enclosure each ant must surrender part of his winter provisions to a sharp-eyed official.

"Why have they left the shelter of the anthill and undertaken this long march? What are they waiting for, motionless and quivering with their gazes turned to a small circle of earth?

"Imagine the shock to our entomologist if he saw five or

ten ants, no different in any way from the others, move forward into the light and amidst an almost religious silence, begin to mime a scene from the life of the ants."

℞

*

A FRIEND of mine had dinner with the president of a large makeup company the other day. It's all fear, the president told him. That's our key word. Keep them afraid that no one will love them and you can sell them anything.

I have pondered this little story. Several years ago I became angry at a friend for questioning a column I wrote for *Southern Living* magazine. "Puss," he said, "what's going on? What's happened to you?" "Nothing," I replied, getting really mad at him. "It's just a magazine article, that's all."

The article was about how I'd gone down to Jackson, Mississippi, to visit my mother and as soon as I got off the airplane she told me I looked like Daisy Mae. I was wearing a short denim skirt and leather sandals and a cotton shirt tied around my waist. Actually, I looked just fine. My hair was long and loose, my skin was clear and the color it turns all by itself in the sun. I looked about as good as I can look.

By week's end I was a different person. Jackson, Mississippi, had done a number on me. I had reverted to type, turned myself back into a frightened sorority girl. I had bought a lot of useless clothes and spent two hundred dollars on makeup and ruined my hair with a permanent.

The magazine article I wrote about all that left the reader with the impression that I thought it was very funny. A lipstick costs eight dollars this year. You have to do a lot of work that someone else thinks up for you to afford that kind of fear.

℞

SUMMER IS THE TIME to deal with paradoxes, with questions that have no answers, problems that can only be surrounded, laid siege to. The Castle of Fat is such a problem. The Castle of Fat is surrounded by a moat of self-deception and absurdities. High walls of fantasy surround it. Evil guards of self-hate man the towers. In the square is an everlasting spring of Diet Coke from which the inhabitants draw sustenance.

Some of my friends and I have set out to besiege the castle. First of all we have to decide whether we are fat or not. I was in conference one afternoon recently with a philosopher and a retired United Airlines pilot. We had been for a long walk around the mountain. Afterwards, we were in the philosopher's kitchen and we were talking about fat.

"I don't know if I'm fat or not," I said. "That's what plagues me. I might not even be fat. I might just think I'm fat."

"The brain has to have glucose," the pilot said. "That's a fact."

"The part I hate," the philosopher said, "the part I cannot deal with, is that a grown man would take off his underpants to weigh himself."

"Correct," the pilot agreed. We sank our chins deep into our hands to think it over.

"Why do you think you're fat?" the pilot asked.

"Because I can't button my skirts," I replied.

"That sounds fat," the philosopher said.

"You could get another skirt," the pilot suggested.

"Stay for dinner," the philosopher's wife put in. "We're having meatloaf and mashed potatoes."

This issue has reached crisis stage in the United States. I know the way I'm thinking about this problem has been imposed on me from without. I can't stand to be dumb and brainwashed about the structure and size of my own body. We will be having further meetings about this matter and I will be giving you reports. One of my characters once said, "I think maybe it is my destiny to start a fad for getting fat."

Then a good-looking carpenter goes by and she decides to wait a few more years before putting her plan into operation.

♈

I'VE BEEN DRIVING along the Natchez Trace, "that old buffalo trail that stretches far into the past." I'm in Chickasaw County, Mississippi, near Cane Creek, moving turtles off the road and thinking about where I'm going and where I've been.

I've been visiting my son Garth, the one that went off to Alaska when he was eighteen. Now he's twenty-eight and he lives on a farm with his wife, Jeannie, and two dogs and three cats and twenty-six cows and five gray horses and two brand-new colts and one lonely guinea hen. There were six guinea hens but foxes killed them so Jeannie and Garth are down to one.

I drove all day yesterday to watch Garth with his animals

and hide out from a lot of sad confused statements being made about me by Arkansas politicians.

I drove to Mississippi to watch Garth with his animals. All his life he has had a way with animals. He can hold out his hand and anything will come to him.

I needed Garth, to touch him and sleep under his roof. He lives in a trailer underneath six enormous oak trees. From his yard all you can see in four directions are fields and trees and skies. Last night the skies were so wonderful — no man-made lights for miles to dim the stars.

The seventeen-year cicadas hatched here last month. Jeannie says it was so loud no one could sleep at night. The guinea hen and the dogs went wild running around gobbling up cicadas like popcorn.

Back in Arkansas the newspapers are full of simplistic versions of a speech I made to the Arkansas governor's school for the gifted and talented. The professional breast-beaters are coming out of the trees like locusts. All I did was tell four hundred fifty students that you had to be able to think for yourself to do creative work. I told them that to achieve that they might have to ignore authorities like their parents and teachers. I was in an especially generous mood that morning and I was trying to show them the full force of my creative self, the part of me that writes the books.

The next thing I knew I was headline news. Thank God for a free press. The stories are calming down and the reporters are printing my side, or as much as I can bring myself to say to defend myself against this tempest in a teapot.

For now, as I stop to write this, I am driving along the Natchez Trace saving turtles in honor of my son Garth's childhood ambition to be the man who builds fences along country roads to save animals from getting run over. I've saved five turtles so far. I stopped one time to save a clump of dirt. A good-looking young man in a red sports car stopped to help me save the fifth turtle. If this was a movie

I was making and the heroine was twenty years younger, I could have made something out of that.

℉

I WAS TEN YEARS OLD the night the Japanese surrendered. It was night in Seymour, Indiana, although it was morning on board the ship where the emissaries of the emperor were signing the papers.

General MacArthur was there, wearing, I was sure, his soft cap and smoking his pipe. And General Skinny Wainwright, who surrendered on Corregidor and spent the war as a Japanese prisoner. If he was skinny before, now he was emaciated. Admiral Halsey was there, and Percival, the Briton who surrendered Singapore. Also, Englishmen, Australians, New Zealanders, Canadians, Russians, Chinese, and row upon row of American sailors in whites. The talks began. The speeches and translations. It meant my uncle would be coming home. He had flown bombers over Germany. Later, he flew with General Claire Chennault and the Flying Tigers. How strange that the youngest and gentlest of my father's brothers should have been the one to drop the bombs.

We had worried about him night and day. Now the worrying was over. I was in bed with my mother and my father and the magic eye of the radio was glowing in the dark and we were listening to the Japanese surrender.

There was no dancing in the streets at 504 Calvin Boulevard in Seymour, Indiana. My parents were very quiet and serious. When I said, "Goody, goody, goody, we beat them," my father said, "Be quiet, war is bad, beginning, middle, and end."

I remember snuggling down into the covers, keeping my elation to myself. Goody, goody, goody, I was thinking. Now they can't come over here and stick bamboo splinters up my fingernails and make me tell everything I know. I had worried myself sick during the war about whether I could stand up under torture. I was afraid they would give me truth serum or the pain would become too great and I would break.

The speeches and translations went on. It was dark in the room but there were stars outside the windows. No more air-raid practices with drawn blinds. Seymour, Indiana, was safe and I could cash in my war bonds. There would never be another war. We had the biggest bomb ever made and no one in the world would ever dare make war on us again. We would divide up the world with Russia and they would run half of it and we would run the other half. Truman and Stalin and Winston Churchill and Ike and General MacArthur would run things and everybody would be happy and have a good time.

The ceremonies ended. "These proceedings are over," General MacArthur said. My father heaved a sigh. We turned off the radio and the magic eye dimmed and went out.

It was some weeks later that Jody Myerson's father came home from the Japanese prisoner-of-war camp. He weighed about a hundred pounds. He looked so terrible I could hardly stand to walk by the house where he was recuperating. "He'll be better," my mother said. "In time he'll be a whole man again." But I had no faith in it. His eyes stared at me through the walls of the house.

I am marked by that war. To this day when I see a group of Japanese businessmen getting on an elevator in New York City I think of Jody's father. I wonder what they think of when they see me stare. It is in spite of such knowledge that I dream of peace.

A LOT OF PEOPLE have gotten the idea that what I do for a living is sit around on a mountain writing a journal. I will answer that, although it is not my nature to explain myself or justify my actions. I do what I think is right and let people think what they please about it. I am not in the business of trying to make people understand my complicated and individual life-style.

What I do is write prose fiction, I write it six or seven hours a day, seven days a week, except for the times when I force myself to stop writing in order not to completely lose touch with the real world. It is easy for me to isolate myself and write books — the hard thing is to live in a real world with other people's needs and desires and dreams. I'm a good receiver — I hear it all.

Anyway, I write for a living. It is an exciting and jealous obsession. One of the ways I fight the obsessive part is by making these journals — they are immediate — out of my immediate experience. Another thing I sometimes reluctantly do is give readings and lectures and very occasionally teach a few days at a college.

But none of this answers the real question. The real question is, How do I have time to write books when other people who wish to be writers don't have time?

I tell students when I talk to them that the first thing a writer has to do is find another source of income. Then, after you have begged, borrowed, stolen, or saved up the money to give you time to write and you spend all of it staying alive while you write, and you write your heart out, after all of that, maybe no one will publish it, and, if they publish it, maybe no one will read it. That is the hard truth. This is what it means to be a writer. I wanted to earn the name of writer for myself and I went to work and did it. I am often awestruck at that fortunate occurrence.

℞

WHEN LAST I wrote about fat, my friends and I were in the philosopher's kitchen trying to decide whether it was wise and/or sane to be so irritated at the body's natural desire to grow larger and to carry stores of food around on top of its muscles and bones. Stores that might come in handy if we lived in a less fortunate country, or if we were survivors of an airplane crash in the Andes or in case the weather should change and no longer favor the great farmlands of the United States of America.

My friends and I have spent many hours this past summer talking very seriously about losing weight. If it is intelligent to give in to the prevailing winds of fashion about how large our bodies should be or become.

How much of our so-called body image is fashion? we asked ourselves. Is it healthy to divest ourselves of pounds? If so, how many? How will we know when to stop?

I am the ringleader of the faction that says, Yes, we must diet. We must to go bed hungry and fit back into our clothes and never give in to inertia and complacence.

So I dieted all summer and in three months I had gained three pounds. Needless to say I do not think this is funny. I think it is very very cruel and unfair.

I was cheered up last night by being taken to hear a young sports nutritionist. She talked to us about food and how we use it and told us about the new studies in nutrition. Telling us a lot of very sensible things about how to become healthy and beautiful without starving ourselves. She kept stressing the importance of complex carbohydrates and exercise and laying off of sugar. The thing she said that cheered me up was that nutritionists are very leery nowadays of people weighing themselves all the time.

We are diverse and wonderful creatures made of starlight

and comet dust. What shape and size our individual bodies take cannot be measured by steel scales and weight charts. We are breathing oxygen created by plants on a planet hurtling through space. We are not a flat image in a mirror or the reflection of a starving model in a fashion magazine. Life is soft and round and generous.

Some of us may be underexercised and over-guilt-ridden but we are not fat. We are wonderful and mysterious and can swim in water.

I WAS TALKING to a reporter the other day and she asked me if I thought my studies in philosophy had affected my writing, shaped the forms I chose to write in. I told her that I didn't separate knowledge into genres or categories because it seemed to me that all of us were probing the same mystery, coming at it from different angles, calling it different things, but all asking the same questions endlessly. Who am I? Why am I here? What are we doing? Is there free will and, if so, how much, and who has it? The scientist and philosopher René Dubos explores these questions with great intelligence and humor. On free will he quotes Samuel Johnson, who said, "All scientific knowledge is against free will, all common sense for it."

I do not understand why I write fiction when the main things I read are books about science and philosophy. Perhaps I think that by exploring character and event I can create actors to act out the questions I am always asking. I have a character named Nora Jane Whittington who lives in Berkeley, California, and who has so much free will that I can't even find out from her whether the twin baby girls she is carrying belong to her old boyfriend, Sandy, or her new boyfriend, Freddy Harwood. I can't finish my new book of stories until Nora Jane agrees to an amniocentesis. She is afraid the needle will penetrate the placenta and frighten the babies.

I created Nora Jane but I have to wait on her to make up her mind before I can finish the title story of my new book. This is a fiction writer's life. Fortunately, I am going to be in California soon and I will drive up to Berkeley and walk around some of Nora Jane's old hangouts. By the time I get home maybe I'll know what to write.

Now I know the answer to the reporter's question. The effect that studying philosophy has had on my fiction writing is that I know that someday I will get to sit down and write a book about Free Will Versus Determinism and the only character will be me.

॰ᵖ

IN ORDER to be a writer you must experience and learn to recognize and cope with periods of what Freeman Dyson calls stuckness. In order to do creative work in any of the arts or sciences you must go through long or short spells of not knowing what is going on, of being irritated, and not being able to find the cause, of being willing to work as hard as you can and what happens isn't valuable enough, isn't good enough, isn't what you meant to do, what you meant to say. Then you just have to keep on working. Then, if you can bear it, if you don't quit and move to Canada or call up Joe and go hiking for two weeks or quit your job or get a divorce or do anything else to relieve the pain, and it is pain, it's really irritating, it puts you in a bad mood, you are irritable to children and can't focus on anything and keep changing your mind, if you can put up with it and just go right on sitting down at that desk every day no matter how much it seems to be an absurd and useless and boring thing to do, the good stuff will suddenly happen. It may be twelve o'clock at night when you're doing something else or are in the bathtub. It will be when you have given up and least expect it. There it will be, the radium, the formula, the good short story, the real poem.

I have the wonderful feeling that I understand this right now, because last night at ten o'clock a two-month stuckness broke and gave me the best new story for my new collection. I had been reading a book called *The Sphinx and the Rainbow.* A wonderful book about the right and left halves of the brain and the frontal lobes. Very clear stuff about how the mind creates the future. How it marshals its forces and then goes to work at its own speed and in ways we cannot always comprehend until the thing is finished. Very rich stuff. I recommend it for anyone, but especially for anyone who is currently stuck.

℘

MY EDITOR has been here and we put together a book of stories. There are thirteen of them. A very slim volume. Thirteen out of twenty were good enough to keep. There is a story that didn't make it called "The Green Tent" about a little boy and his grandmother who travel all over the universe in a tent. I'm sorry I had to give that one up. I really liked that story.

Hemingway said one of the great problems for a writer is deciding who his audience will be. Do you write for the reviewers, terrified they will call something cute or sentimental? If they manage to scare you enough you will get to the point where you are afraid to write about anything really human, like passion or love. People are endlessly fascinated by love. They talk about it and laugh about it and desire and hate it. Whenever one of us falls in love our friends watch it as they would the progress of a disease.

So I have written a book of stories called *Drunk With Love* in which I set out to explore what I know about the subject. I have failed. Not failed as a writer. But I have learned nothing about love and added nothing to our store of understanding.

"All is clouded by desire, like a mirror by smoke." I thought I was going to penetrate that mystery through my characters. Wrong. All I did was wade deeper and deeper into the mystery. In the end I let the last words of the book be spoken by Nora Jane Whittington's unborn babies.

"Let's be quiet," Tammili said. "Okay," Lydia replied.

God bless my editor. He let me keep that in.

"What are you going to do now?" he asked, when we had finished our work.

"I think I'll go fall in love," I answered.

"Why don't you just go home and stick your finger in an electric wall socket instead," he suggested. "It would save you the trouble of getting dressed up."

He's right. I've changed my mind about going to stick my finger in the electric wall socket of love. I'm going down to New Orleans instead and get my grandchildren and go riding around in my little blue car pretending we are space cadets. I'll let someone younger and braver than I am sit around the house waiting for the phone to ring.

℘

I RECENTLY SAW a wonderful sight. I was driving back from New Orleans and stopped in Pass Manchac, Louisiana, to see how things looked now that the flood waters had receded. Pass Manchac is a famous place on the Bonnet Carre Spillway across from New Orleans. It is a small fishing village that was several feet underwater in the October floods. I saw it then with water all over the floors of the houses and men walking along the railroad tracks carrying sandbags, still trying to save what could be saved.

Anyway, the flood was several weeks ago and I stopped by to see how things were going and went into Sykes' grocery store and talked to the proprietor and had some doughnuts and bought a tablet and a pencil. The tablet was slightly mildewed on the edges. The proprietor told me about filling the sandbags, who all was there and who came to help and we discussed how resilient men and women are. Then she turned around. "Oh, look at this," she said. A great mountain of a man was coming in the door. A beautiful tanned man with white hair leading or being led by two small children. The proprietor told me that the smallest one had been abused so badly he had to be in a full body cast for six months. "That's their foster father," she said. "He's got them now and they're okay."

They were beautiful children. They came into the store and got some candy and went to the back to find life preservers as they were going out on a boat for a Sunday outing.

"Hold me," the small child said, as soon as he saw me looking at him. I picked him up in my arms and held him there. "We're getting to adopt them in February," the big fisherman said. "It's all set."

"Oh, that's great," the proprietor said, and for a moment

I had a sense of sharing the community of Pass Manchac, a fishing village where people know each other and are involved in each other's lives and stories.

I am haunted by these events. For many miles down the road, I was filled with a sense of elation. The story of mankind is not written in the occasional crazy parent who will harm his own child. The story of mankind is the big fisherman who comes along and sets things right . . . the physicians and surgeons and nurses in some emergency room who are working the night shift and are there when the broken child arrives and put him back together and the fisherman who gathers the child into his life and goes to work to love him and the proprietor who cleans up the store after the flood and sells me a slightly mildewed tablet at half price to write this on.

I AM COMPELLED to write about this even though it embarrasses me to keep talking about my grandchildren. Still, this is supposed to be a writer's journal and if there is one thing I've learned about writing it is to follow your compulsions.

Here is what I am compelled to write about today.

I have been alone for thirty-eight hours with two small children and no car. I have been locked up in an apartment with a four-year-old boy and a one-and-a-half-year-old girl and I am here to report that taking care of small children is the single most exciting, complicated, difficult, creative, and maddening job on the green earth.

Finally, I called for help. That famous seventy-seven-year-old child-worshipper I have told you about, my mother, is

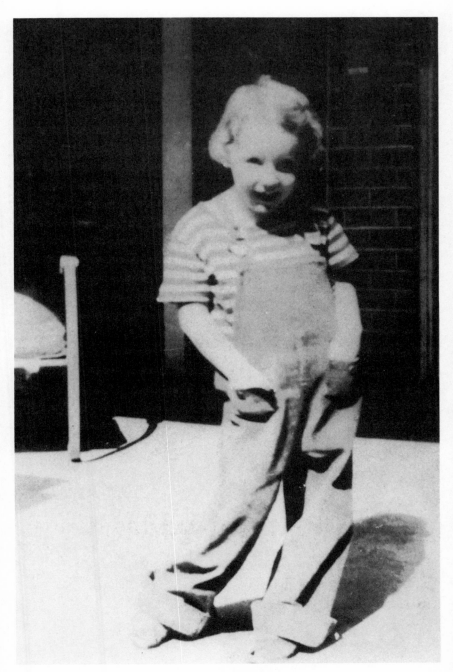

Ellen on sleeping porch, Hopedale Plantation

Ellen on Dixie, friends

Ellen and Dooley, 1939

Hopedale Plantation, built around 1905

Ellen and mother,
1939 or 1940

Friend, Dooley, Ellen,
Aunt Roberta Alford
(Indiana during war)

Ellen and Dooley

Ellen visiting in New Orleans, taken in booth in French Quarter, summer of 1948

Cynthia Jane Hancock (Ellen's best friend) and Ellen outside Horace Mann School in sixth grade. Early spring, Harrisburg, Illinois

Mother, Ellen, Father, Dooley, 1939

Ellen, 1950

Ellen, seventh grade

Ellen at Columbia Military Academy dance, Columbia, Tennessee, 1951

Ellen at Chi Omega house dance at Vanderbilt or University of Alabama or Southern Seminary

Purple Clarion staff, Harrisburg High School, 1950. Ellen as feature editor

Mack Harness, Ellen,
1984

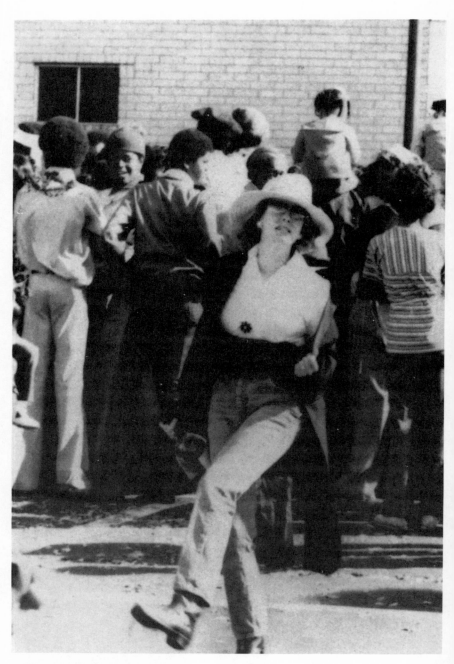

Ellen at Mardi Gras, 1976

Ellen's sons at her fourth
wedding

Ellen's sons: Marshall Walker, Garth Walker, Pierre Walker

Rosalie Davis, to whom *In the Land of Dreamy Dreams* is dedicated only ten blocks away, so I called and invited her to come pick us up and go with us to the mall to buy some winter clothes for the children. She's always up for a good time so she came right over and got us and we went to the store. I had it in my mind to buy them some socks and jackets and something nice to wear in case we got invited to a party.

Two and a half hours later the four of us emerged from the mall and began to search for the car. "I'm too old for this," the child-worshipper said. "This is one generation too many."

We had purchased a pair of Superman pajamas with a Velcro cape and a package of T-shirts that might someday fit someone and we had left a children's department in tatters. Only the unbelievable patience of a saleslady named Laverne had made it possible for us to purchase anything.

The child-worshipper took us home and declined my invitation to come in. Later, I allowed the four-year-old to watch a Care Bears movie four times in a row — and that after all my tirades against children watching television. It was a movie called *The Care Bears in the Land without Feelings*. By bedtime he had mastered all the parts and had chosen for himself the role of Professor Coldheart. "THAT'S WHAT YOU GET FOR BEING SO TENDERHEARTED," he kept telling me. "SO MUCH FOR LOVE AND TENDERNESS AND LITTLE FUZZY WUZZIES."

The sun fell below the horizon. We had some cereal and milk. We dressed for bed. The child-worshipper called to see how we were getting along.

"How's it going?" she said.

"How did I do this?" I said. "How did I do this day after day?"

"You weren't very good at it," she answered. "It never was your long suit."

HERE IS my Christmas carol.

The best thing that has happened to me so far this holiday season was a discussion I had at the drugstore with two women who work there. The three of us decided that there was no way we were going into debt for Christmas. No way we were going to wake up on January first with a lot of bills to pay. God bless you, Merry Gentlemen, sell this plastic junk to someone else. You won't sell it to Libby and Darlene and me.

"What do you want for Christmas?" I asked Libby as I was leaving. "I want grocery stores and drugstores to stop putting candy by the checkout counter," she said. "So children scream for it while their mothers wait to pay. What do you all want?"

"I want folks to stop selling dope to kids," Darlene said. "My doctor at the clinic, he's got his only son locked up with his brain dead from taking dope. My doctor was crying when he was seeing me. Imagine that."

The three of us hung our heads over the idea of anyone selling dope to children. We Three Kings of Orient Are. Three wise women at the Katz & Bestoff Drug Store.

Well, this is the saddest time of year and everyone knows it. Adeste Fideles. O come, all ye faithful. Everyone suffers the winter equinox, the death of the year. Everyone knows the sadness of Christmas afternoon after the presents are opened and the dinner eaten and there's nothing left to do but pretend you had a good time.

One Christmas, I stayed all alone on a mountain and didn't eat anything all day while Christmas went on below me. I was the Grinch of Christmas and it was one of the best days of my life. I wrote the last chapter of a novel and wouldn't even answer the phone.

You'll lose all your fans if you start knocking Christmas, the voice of bah humbug cautions me. Not my readers, I answer. My readers are literate people who can think for themselves. They are people who write me letters I like to read and tell me things I want to know.

So here is a Merry Christmas to all my friends and all the people who have helped me make these essays by doing the things I wrote about, and to all the little children screaming and crying for candy at the checkout stands and to all the parents who give in and to all those who say no.

℞

I WENT TO the inauguration of the Radio Reading Service for the Blind and Print Handicapped Citizens of the state of Mississippi. There was a party at ten o'clock in the morning in the Mississippi Public Broadcasting studios and most of the writers in the state were there to start things off by reading from their books. This is a service that will go out day after day to all those who cannot see or are unable to hold a book or turn a page.

It was a bright January morning and everyone looked grand in winter suits and dress-up dresses. The director and manager of the service were there, looking properly nervous and excited. There was an opening ceremony with members of the legislature and doctors and lawyers and actresses and other volunteer readers. There was fierce competition for those spots. Mississippi is not a state where a chance to be on stage is taken lightly.

After the ceremony we all trooped over to the studios and the recording sessions began. Eudora Welty led off with her haunting and beautiful story "A Worn Path." The rest of us were in the anteroom listening on a scratchy desk radio. The minute Miss Welty's soft enchanting voice came on the air things changed in the room and the magic of storytelling was upon us.

"It was December," she read, "— a bright frozen day in the early morning. Far out in the country there was an old Negro woman with her head tied in a red rag, coming along a path through the pinewoods. Her name was Phoenix Jackson. She was very old and small and she walked slowly in the dark pine shadows, moving a little from side to side in her steps, with the balanced heaviness and lightness of a pendulum in a grandfather clock."

Miss Welty was followed by Willie Morris and Ellen Douglas and Gloria Norris and Richard Ford and Luke Wallin and Charlotte Capers and Carroll Case and Felder Rushing and Patrick Smith, some on tape and some in person. In the midst of this excitement a troop of sighted sixth-graders passed through the room with a string of blind and print-handicapped fifth-graders in tow. They were being led by a wonderful-looking little redhead in a plaid dress. She weaved her way in between Eudora Welty and Ellen Douglas and a pair of senators. "Excuse me," she said. "Excuse me, please," and led her charges back to tour the studios which would produce the books they would be hearing.

In a world of television watchers it is nice for a writer to know there is an audience who still needs words unaccompanied by pictures other than the ones they make up in their own minds.

SOME TIME AGO I decided to leave the secluded life where I wrote my books and go out into the world and see what was going on.

*   *   *

I spent two weeks on a reading tour. First I went to Boulder, Colorado, and read a story to the students and had a wonderful time walking around in the snow. Then I flew to Minneapolis–Saint Paul to read a story in the beautiful Walker Art Center. Outside, only a few blocks away, seven hundred volunteer workers were putting the finishing touches on the Ice Palace. In the dead of winter, in one of the coldest cities in the world, seven hundred grown men and women have cut blocks of ice out of a frozen lake and built a palace one hundred and twenty-eight feet high.

Minneapolis is always full of wonders for me. The Walker Art Center was showing the fifteen-and-a-half-hour film, *Heimat,* by the German director Edgar Reitz. It is one of the most beautiful movies I have seen in years. The story of a small German village and its inhabitants from the end of World War One to the present.

On Sunday, I flew home to Jackson, Mississippi, and changed suitcases and drove to Shreveport, Louisiana, to read a story to the officers' wives at the Barksdale Air Force Base. Headquarters of the Eighth Air Force of the Strategic Air Command. I was taken on a tour of the base by two of the pilots' wives. We went to see the sheds where uniformed men were standing on ladders working on the engines of the twenty-five-year-old B-52s and I marveled at the design of the KC-135s that fuel them in the air. I spent the day with the wives of the men who are keeping America safe. Their business is peace, they told me, and I believed them and thanked them for it.

There are many wonders outside the egocentric little cave where books are written. I have found out that the Federal Reserve system isn't part of the federal government and now I've been to visit a SAC base. There's no telling what will happen next.

℞

WRITERS HATE to be questioned. It's an almost superstitious feeling that it's wrong to probe or analyze the muse. And yet, sometimes things come to light from questions.

In a question-and-answer session at the University of Colorado I found myself articulating something I have been suspecting for a long time.

How do you create characters? a student asked. How do you keep thinking up new people to tell your stories? I may not be able to anymore, I answered. I've been writing for about ten years now and I have created a cast of characters that are like a Fellini troupe. They are always trying to steal the spotlight away from each other.

It's gotten to the point where it's impossible for me to create new characters because the old ones keep grabbing up all the roles. The minute I think up a new dramatic situation, one of my old characters grabs it up and runs with it. Minor characters get up off the page and take the pen out of my hand and start expanding their roles. Scenes that have no business in the stories sprout like mushrooms as Freddy Harwood or Nieman interrupt stories to give themselves daring adventures or heroic moments.

In a way my characters are right. I can see their point. I have a responsibility to Freddy Harwood to let him tell his side of the story and not just leave him sitting in a hot tub with a broken heart.

Also, I am beginning to suspect there may be a limited number of characters any one writer can create and perhaps a limited number of stories any writer can tell. Perhaps that's how we know when to quit and find something else to do for a living. I live in horror that I won't know when to quit. I don't want to be one of those writers who run out of things to write and then go around the rest of their lives talking about writing but not really producing anything anyone wants to read. When I've told all my stories and created all my characters I want to get off the stage as quickly as I can and with as much grace as possible.

℘

SOME TIME AGO I had just finished a draft of a novel and left it in my typist's tennis racket cover and then gone barreling down the highway leading south out of the Ozark Mountains.

I was driving down the highway eating powdered dough-nuts and stopping every now and then to write things down. At the end of that journal entry I realized it was an illusion that the novel was finished and I knew very well it would take several more years and two or three more drafts to finish it.

Now I am working on it again. The *Anabainein,* I call this strange creation. A going up, a journey to the interior. It is a novel set in Greece during the Peloponnesian Wars. My pet book, based on a story I made up when I was a child. My mother loved the classics and filled my head with stories of the Greek pantheon and the glories of fifth-century Athens, and I made up a story about a slave girl who is raised by a philosopher and allowed to learn to read and write.

All these characters, all this research, all these pages and pages and pages. Perhaps it will be the best thing I have ever written. Perhaps the worst. Still, I have to finish it. A poet once told me that the worst thing a writer can do is fail to finish the things he starts. It was a long time before I knew what that meant or why it was true. The mind is trying very hard to tell us things when we write books. The first impulse is as good as the second or the third — any thread if followed long enough will lead out of the labyrinth and into the light. So I believe or choose to believe.

The work of a writer is to create order out of chaos. Always, the chaos keeps slipping back in. Underneath the created order the fantastic diversity and madness of life goes on, expanding and changing and insisting upon itself. Still, each piece contains the whole. Tell one story truly and with clarity and you have done all anyone is required to do.

I AM SPENDING the winter thinking about money. About money as a concept, an act of faith, a means of conveyance. Also, I am thinking about plain old money, the kind we are greedy for and think will solve our problems. Maybe it will solve our problems. It gives us the illusion of security. Money in the bank, a nest egg, something to fall back upon. Yes, I am going to ask money to forgive me for all the nasty things I've said about it.

I began my study of money by watching "Wall Street Week." I started watching it for a joke. It amused me to see how happy and cheerful the people on "Wall Street Week" always are. No underweight actors and actresses begging the audience for love. Not this bunch. These are well-dressed, normal-sized, very confident people. All will be well, "Wall Street Week" assures me. The market goes up and the market comes back down, but after all, it's only a game. The great broker in the sky smiles benignly down on his happy children.

Why not? I began to say to myself. Who am I to sneer at

all this good clean fun? So I bought some stocks and now I really have a reason to watch "Wall Street Week." Figures appear on the screen, bulls and bears made their predictions. Bulls and bears. Now I know what that means. Bulls are good things that mean I'm making money. Bears are bad things that mean I've made a bad mistake.

To paraphrase a poet, the Dow Jones Industrial Average rises and falls and thy name, O God, is kept before the public.

What a wonderful new obsession. At last I understand capitalism. At last my father and I have something to talk about. Once, years ago, my father begged me with tears in his eyes to take a course in the stock market. I agreed and signed up for a class. Alas, at the very first class meeting I fell in love with a redheaded engineer from Kansas and we went off into the night and never found time to come back to the class. Each age has its rewards. Once I had love and romance. Now I have the Dow Jones Industrial Average and the "Wall Street Week in Review."

I HAVE BEEN OFF at a writers' conference in Grand Forks, in the beautiful farmland of northeastern North Dakota. Where a fellow Mississippian named Johnny Little has just staged the seventeenth annual University of North Dakota Writers' Conference.

Johnny is an old colleague of mine from a class Eudora Welty taught at Millsaps College in 1967. He was born in Raleigh, Mississippi, where he was the smartest boy in town. Then Johnny went to Millsaps and got even smarter. Then he went up to Fayetteville, Arkansas, to make a writer, as he calls it. Then off to North Dakota to teach. The winters were long and cold and he got so lonesome he started a southern writers' conference, which turned into a national, then an international, affair. For seventeen years Johnny has been luring writers from all over the world up to Grand Forks to lend a hand in celebrating the spring thaw.

Edward Albee, James Dickey, Gregory Corso, Truman Capote, Susan Sontag, Jim Whitehead, Tom Wolfe, Joseph Brodsky, the list is long and illustrious. The University of North Dakota Annual Spring Thaw Southern and International Writers' Conference. Not to be confused with the Raleigh, Mississippi, Tobacco Spit and Logrolling Contest, another of Johnny's pet projects.

I had a good time being there but I never worked so hard at being a writer. It seemed to me I was being interviewed or questioned every waking moment by some bright young man or woman. I can't even remember all the advice I gave.

> *To make a prairie it takes a clover and one bee,*
> *One clover, and a bee,*
> *And revery.*
> *The revery alone will do,*
> *If bees are few.*

That poem by Emily Dickinson was supposed to be the theme of the conference but the only time I heard anyone say anything about a prairie was a joke someone told about the flatness of the land around Grand Forks. Nothing to see, and nothing to get in the way of seeing it. I flew home down the course of the Mississippi River and then over to Shreveport, Louisiana, to address the Louisiana Library Association. If you are wondering how I am getting any serious writing done under these circumstances you are not alone. The dour old Scot who rules the roost in my subconscious is very suspicious when I tell him that seeing the world is part of a writer's work.

HERE IS a writing lesson. I'm not much good as a regular writing teacher. I only know things as they happen, at the time they happen. If I knew them all the time I could get up every morning and write a masterpiece. The Greeks got up every morning and wrote masterpieces. Euripides wrote eighty-eight plays, of which nineteen survive. His fellow Greeks liked his plays so much that prisoners could gain their freedom by learning to recite them.

But this is supposed to be a writing lesson. Here is how I write a book. First I get a wonderful idea and I drop everything I'm doing and go and write it down and expand it as much as I can. Then I get very excited and go off and eat some ice cream or something I usually deny myself. Four or five days later I go back and read what I wrote and I decide it's pretty good, but not as good as I dreamed it would be. A few days later the story or characters I began to create will begin to haunt me; they want another chance to show they are as wonderful as I originally thought they were and I go back into the story and begin to work on it. Work means exactly that. Hard thinking and hard attention and walking around the house with the telephone off the hook and the bed unmade. Trying to remember what happens next. It is more like memory than imagination. The imagination part only happens in bursts of excitement — it happens when it gets ready to happen. Days go by while I work and work and work, and, for some reason, which I have never been able to understand, I am able to put up with this very hard, boring part of writing. Meanwhile I take good care of myself. I sleep at regular hours and eat as intelligently as I can and maybe even clean up the house and buy some flowers for the table. The book is writing itself while these things go on. Then one morning, it was this morning for me for this book, it breaks open, like a flower opening or a storm cloud, and it all makes perfect sense and I know how to write down what I have dreamed or imagined. I know what happens next and what the characters are thinking and how they dance with each other on the page. If it is a short story or a poem two or three of these episodes will do to complete the piece. If it is a novel only Athena knows how long it will take or how many spells of hard, boring, seemingly useless work followed by bursts of illumination must go on before the plot is woven and the book finished.

A piece of writing is the product of a series of explosions in the mind. It is not the first burst of excitement and its aftermath. It is helpful to me to pretend that writing is like building a house. I like to go out and watch real building projects and study the faces of the carpenters and masons as they add board after board and brick after brick. It reminds me of how hard it is to do anything really worth doing.

ℂℙ

I'M NOT A bad person. If I see a turtle on the road, I stop and pick it up and return it to the grass. I know the universe is one. I know it's all one reality. So why does it make me so furious, why do I want to kill and kill and kill when the turtles on the pond kill the baby ducks? They killed seven in April and five more in May and they are at it again.

Edmund Wilson once wrote a great short story on this subject, called "The Man Who Hated Snapping Turtles." I could have written that story. I wouldn't have had to invent a character. I could have used myself. One morning I wake up and there are five brand-new beautiful soft fluffy baby ducks following their mother out from behind a grass nest and walking side by side to the water. They enter the water without sound. They glide like angels. The mother looks like my beautiful daughter-in-law Rita. The baby ducks are my grandchildren. A turtle rears its head. Kill, I'm screaming. The neighbors are on their porches. They know what's going on. We have all been sharing the tragedy of the ducks.

Kill, I'm screaming. Doesn't anybody have a gun? I grab an empty Coke bottle and run out onto the pier and throw it at the turtle. Success. It scares him off for the moment. Get those babies back on the land, I'm screaming at the large ducks. Don't you know what's good for you? Can't you protect your young?

I can't stand it. Here we are in the sovereign state of Mississippi and we are helpless to prevent those ducks from getting killed. How am I going to travel and see the world? What's going to happen when I get to Mexico or India? Get back in the bushes, I'm yelling at the ducks. We'll drain the pond. We'll kill all the turtles in the world. What am I supposed to do? I can't stay in the house and never go out on the porch. I can't keep the drapes closed so I'll forget the pond is there. It's there. The baby ducks are on the pond and the turtles are coming to get them.

STUCK IN THE very heart of summer in the middle of a heat wave and I'm sitting here trying to write this book. Why did I ever start this book? What on earth possessed me to think I could write an historical novel? I remember when I started it. I woke up one beautiful fall morning in Fayetteville,

Arkansas, and decided I had missed my calling. I should have been a scholar, I said to myself. I should have kept on learning Greek.

I will write a novel set in ancient Greece, I told myself. Anyone can do anything, and I am going down the hill and go to the library and take out every book ever written about ancient Greece and read them and then I'm going over to Daniel Levine's office and borrow all his books and then I'll sign up for Greek classes and I will spend as many years as it takes. I want to be a great and honored writer, a scholar, a serious and noble person.

So I put on my hiking shoes and walked down the mountain and on down to Dickson Street and marched into the library and began. That first month was wonderful. No more the unstructured life of a fiction writer. No more ego. No more taking real life and twisting it into character and scenes and devising plots and opening lines. All I had to do now was sit all day in a little cubby at the university library and read and take notes. I was wearing an old tweed skirt and an oxford cloth shirt and brown brogans and knee socks. My horn-rimmed glasses. At exactly eleven o'clock every morning I would walk over to the student union and eat doughnuts and drink coffee. Who cared if I got fat? I was a scholar now. Lost in the stacks.

Everything was going fine. My time schedule called for me to read and study for five years before I began to write.

I was covering yellow legal pads with knowledge of the past. Plants and herbs, ancient weapons, walled cities, how to mix mortar, how to make cloth, the clothes people wore, their music and sculpture and plays.

Then one morning I stayed home and sat at a sunlit table in a dining room overlooking the mountains and began to read the notes. I was in the dining room. I wasn't in my crowded messy workroom where I am a writer. I was in a sunlit dining room being a scholar. Suddenly an old story I had made up when I was a child began to appear on the page. A story about a young Greek girl who saves an abandoned infant. Suddenly that old unconscious story, about saving, of course, who else, myself, came rising up and I was writing and writing and writing all day.

I wrote for three or four days. That writing is still the best part of the novel. I may never again write pages as good as those. And here I am, four years later, on the fourth or fifth or sixth or seventh draft of the cursed thing and still writing and still studying and it isn't finished yet.

This is what a writer's life is really like. Calling up my editor and my agent nearly every day to get stroked and reassured. Walking around my house blaming the book on everyone I know and scared to death I can't finish it and scared to death it isn't any good. "I would never encourage anyone to be a writer," Eudora Welty once said to me. "It's too hard. It's just too hard to do."

THE INGRATE, part one, or, I have had too much of the rich harvest I myself desired. I am sick of being a writer. Not of writing. Not of the wonderful mystical thing I do all alone in a messy little room I call an office. Not the inspiration, the conception, the writing down of poems and essays and stories. Black ink onto yellow paper, magic. But I am sick of answering questions and signing my name and being loved by strangers. "But I am tired of applepicking now, I have had too much of the great harvest I myself desired."

Maybe it was that one really nasty irresponsible review. Maybe it is being misunderstood and misinterpreted that drives writers crazy and makes them go off to the hills to brood and pout and stop talking to people. Sixth-grade politics. Fourth-grade emotions. Second-grade sensitivity.

So now I am holed up back in Jackson, Mississippi, with the phone off the hook and the television turned to the wall and I am thinking. I have contracts for three books. I have a wonderful assignment from *Southern Magazine* to go up to the White River and freeze to death camping out with my boyfriend at Thanksgiving. I have three children and three grandchildren, all in perfect health. My new book is selling well despite the *New York Times*. I work for the best radio program in the United States of America. I live in the greatest silliest wildest country that ever raised a flag on a flagpole. And I'll be all right as soon as I get some rest.

Yesterday I was talking on the phone to a writer, and she asked, "Are you writing anything?" And I said, "Of course not." And she said, "Well, that's publication."

IT IS IMPOSSIBLE to be stupid while listening to Bach. There is something about the art of fugue that soothes the brain. I used to make a joke about this and tell my friends they could stop suffering love if they would stop listening to love songs and listen to Bach instead.

Recently, in the middle of a rainy Sunday afternoon while I was lounging around on the sofa in the middle of a pile of books, worrying about my children and getting my mind in a tangle with this or that imagined catastrophe, I came upon a chapter in a book of Lewis Thomas's essays in which he explores the proposition that he could go to the scientists of the world and ask them for the answers to three questions.

The first would concern the strange mind-reading abilities of honeybees.

The second question would be about music. "Surely

music," Doctor Thomas says, "along with ordinary language, is as profound a problem for human biology as can be thought of, and I would like to see something done about it. What music is, why it is indispensable for human existence, what music really means. Hard questions like that."

"Why is the art of fugue so important and what does this single piece of music do to the human mind?"

As soon as I read that I put down the book, went to the closet where I store my records, found a Bach recording, put it on the stereo, and by the third musical phrase the tangles in my mind were unwound and I knew what to do next. The piece I was listening to was Bach's Prelude and Fugue in C Major, perhaps the most beautiful piece of music in the world.

I never did find out what the third question would be.

I WOKE THIS MORNING dreaming of the woods. An opening in a line of trees seemed to lead deeper and deeper into the woods, perhaps to a pasture, perhaps to a river. Tall pine and oak and sycamore trees arching above me and a small road of pine straw and fallen leaves to walk upon, a golden mattress of a road. It was very still, the very heart of the woods, and I was alone there and perfectly quiet and perfectly happy. Some weeks ago *Southern Magazine* asked me where I would like to go in the South, what I would like to investigate and learn about and praise. "The rivers," I answered without thinking, without having to pause to think. Wherever there are rivers and trees I am happy there. I have lived too long to trust the places man has spoiled and changed and bought and sold. They have failed me every one. I cannot even remember the names of the resorts I have gone to with my rich husbands, the sadness and drunkenness and disorder of those places. But the woods. I remember every river I have ever set out upon, every pond and lake and swimming hole, every forbidden borrow pit, every tree I ever climbed or leaned into or loved. "I will go to a river," I told the editor of the magazine. "It won't cost much to send me where I'm going. If only I can find my tent."

"Which river?" he asked.

"Somewhere in Arkansas," I answered. "In the Ozarks. Let me call my guide and get out maps and I'll get back to you."

Of all the people I have ever gone camping and river-hunting with the one who suits me best is a young man from Fayetteville, Arkansas, named Mack Harness. I call him the Trout Fisherman. He calls me the Famous Writer. We get along in the woods. I trust him not to let me get killed and he trusts me to get sullen when he smokes. It's a nice arrangement and we have been camping out and hunting rivers and admiring trees and rocks and waterfalls together for about seven years. So I called up the Trout Fisherman and asked him to come down to Jackson and help me. He flew down and we spent a weekend looking at maps and eating roast beef sandwiches and Oreo cookies and vanilla ice cream. About ten o'clock on Sunday morning, while listening to *The Well-Tempered Clavier,* we came up with something we liked.

"Let's go up here," I said, pointing a finger to a place on a map southeast of Fayetteville and somewhat west of Memphis. "Let's go find the source of the White River."

"Looking for the White," he said. "That's great."

"Where is this?" I asked. "Here, take the magnifying glass. Goddamnit, we've got to get some better maps. We need some geological survey maps. Here is where it should be. Right here."

"That's up by Venus Mountain. We can find that."

"We've got to go to wherever it rises. Even if it ends up being in Missouri."

"When are we going?"

"The week before Thanksgiving. I can't get away till then."

"It's going to be cold."

"I know. Well, you're tough."

"That I am," he said, and walked out on the balcony to smoke a cigarette.

November 16, 1986.

I can't wait. The woods are there and the Ozark Mountains and the rivers so cold and clear and moving so fast. Calm down, I tell myself. They have been there a long time. They'll be there when you get there. And you can make a fire and sleep in your tent. If I can find my tent. When last seen it was in my son's apartment in Fayetteville, Arkansas. It had better be there when I get there *with no holes in it* if he ever wants to borrow it again. What else do we need for a river trip? Some health food. Fritos and Nacho Cheese Flavored Doritos, Vienna sausage and rat cheese and soda crackers and chocolate chip cookies and chewing gum (in case anybody decides to stop smoking).

November 16.

The Trout Fisherman will fly down to Jackson on November 20 and on the twenty-first we will drive up through the Mississippi Delta, through the deltas of the Yazoo, then the Sunflower, then the Mississippi (where I was born) and across the Mississippi to the Arkansas Delta (where the Trout Fisherman was born).

We will cross the river at Vicksburg and ride up the Arkansas side to Lake Village, the most beautiful town in the world, and on up to Pine Bluff, which has been ruined by paper mills and an arsenal for binary nerve gas, then on to Little Rock where we will tip our hat to the editor of *Southern*

Magazine who put us up to this and is paying for the Oreos and Fritos and Nacho Cheese Flavored Doritos and Vienna sausage and soda crackers and gasoline and camera film and, God forbid, the Camel cigarettes.

November 21.

Bad news and a change of plans. The Trout Fisherman has had a death in his family and now will meet me in Fayetteville the Monday before Thanksgiving. So much for our drive up through the deltas, but we've done that before and will do it again in a happier season.

For now I will fly up alone on Monday and we'll find our tent and head out on Wednesday morning. The tent will only be an icon now. The Ark of the Tent. The Tent of All Tents will spend the week rolled up in the back of the Isuzu and we will go find the source of the river and return to spend the night in the Designated Driver's geodesic dome near Goshen, Arkansas, which looks down four hundred feet onto a beautiful S-curve of the river and the fields it feeds and guards. We will sleep near water in this house the Trout Fisherman helped the Designated Driver build. "We are getting soft," I told the Trout Fisherman. "I know," he answered. "Well, that's how it falls for now."

Since we were ruined anyway we decided to get really decadent and spent the evening seeing a double feature. We saw *Peggy Sue Got Married*. Took a Coke break and went back in for *Star Trek IV*.

November 24. Jackson, Mississippi, Airport, 9:00 A.M. waiting.

Leaving Jackson in a hard gray rain. Cold, straight rain with flash flood warnings. I hate to fly in weather like this. Also, I hate to leave my work as I was writing well, working on *The Anna Papers*.

But a writer has to make a living. Also, a writer has to have some fun or the work gets cold. This may be too much fun. Since September I've been on twenty-eight airplanes. Well, two more takeoffs and landings and I'll be in Fayetteville, pick up a four-wheel-drive Isuzu, meet the Trout Fisherman and the Designated Driver, and I'll be on my way.

10:53. Takeoff.

Always a holy moment. We are flying a Northwest Airlines Saab Fairchild 253, made in Sweden, land of the gorgeous Socialists.

Notes on plane: Good title for book, *Principles of Flight*. The Pearl River below me shrouded in mist, wreathed in clouds. So beautiful. Tall pines and orange-leaved oaks along its banks, cold gray water. Eudora's river. She made it famous in the lovely short story "The Wide Net." Also, her character King McClain left his hat on the banks of the Big Black and some say he died and others say he ran away. Rivers. So wonderful to know and love the rivers of your state.

Flying over Mississippi at ten thousand feet in bad bumpy weather I think about my ancestors who came here on boats down the Monongahela and the Allegheny to the Ohio and on down the Mississippi to Natchez and Mayersville. What would they think if they could see me now, daring to complain about anything?

We are approaching the Sunflower River. I can see it below me through the rain. I am wearing a soccer shirt, khaki skirt, boots, and an old raincoat one of my teenagers outgrew and left behind.

Above Greenwood things got so beautiful I could hardly bear it. Small scattered featherlike clouds above a winding chocolate-brown river. The multicolored trees of Mississippi, cold and shrouded with mist, water oak, sycamore, maple, pine, dogwood, and persimmon.

We landed in Memphis in a downpour and let some folks off and took some more on and took off again for Fayetteville. I am getting excited now. Going home, I have promised

John Dacus at Hayes and Sanders Bookstore to be there at four for a book signing. It looks like I am going to make it after all.

5:00: The Trout Fisherman shows up at the bookstore wearing a coat and tie. "I'm ready," he says. "Sign my book." "So am I," I answer, and write my initials on his wrist. [Some people never grow up.]

November 25.

Fayetteville. Tuesday: Cold wet misty weather. One more day and we will leave to find the river. Perhaps the weather will clear by then and we will have a good day for the expedition. The Trout Fisherman and I are camped at the Mountain Inn where the big news is that there has been an accident at the Fayetteville water plant and no one can drink the water. Strange and prophetic that even in this remote mountain town the water is not safe. Too many people in one place. Any Indian could tell you that. The Trout Fisherman is part Cherokee, he becomes diminished when he stays too long in cities, as I do.

When we checked into the hotel the desk clerk handed us each a gallon of bottled water and we carried them to our rooms.

Later: It is raining cats and dogs. The Trout Fisherman left in a deluge to retrieve the four-wheel-drive Isuzu from the repair shop. He returned two and a half hours later with bad news. He had stopped off to shoot pool at Roger's Pool Hall. It was dark when he came out and the lights wouldn't work on the Isuzu. We decided to try to get them fixed in the morning even though it might give us a later start. Perhaps I will get to unroll the green tent after all. I went to sleep dreaming of what we would find. A spring trickling out of the ground, disturbing the leaves somewhere halfway up a hill. Would there be a marker? There was none noted on the map. People in Arkansas are good about leaving things alone. Perhaps there would be nothing there but water.. I went to sleep with water beating on the panes outside the windows of my room, falling down gullies and ravines in my dreams.

November 27: Making Our Own Fun, Or, Why Are We Always So Crazy?

5:30: Woke up. Argued about the lights on the Isuzu.

5:45: Trout Fisherman goes out to work on lights on the Isuzu. No luck.

6:10: Called Trout Fisherman's brother. Tried to borrow a truck. No luck. He was driving it to Shreveport.

6:30: Packed Isuzu. Ate breakfast (bacon, eggs, toast, pancakes, hash browns, coffee, syrup). Got in a remarkably good creative mood.

7:00: Drove Isuzu to Jim Ray Pontiac where a masterful service manager understood our problem, mobilized a team of mechanics, and had us on our way with a new light switch in fifteen minutes. *I love Fayetteville.* Where else will people take writing a story that seriously? Where else will people try to save you money while they sell you something? Salespeople in Fayetteville were always doing that for me when I lived there, pointing out bargains, telling me to wait for the sale, helping me curb my extravagant Delta ways.

November 27.

We are on our way. So much water. Rain and mist and clouds, a cold wet misty freezing thoroughly gray day. Perfect morning to go searching for a place where four rivers rise.

We drive out past Goshen to pick up the Designated Driver who lives in a dome overlooking the White River just below Beaver Lake. The Designated Driver is Dave Tucker, an old friend who makes his living as a commercial artist and illustrator. He is also, not incidentally, one of the best jazz and fusion drummers in the Ozarks and played rock and roll with the Trout Fisherman's band in their high school days. It's a good crew. It's going to be a good trip. We can feel it in our bones.

We inspect the river from Dave's balcony. Then we go down the long gravel road and out onto Highway 45, backtrack past Goshen and find Highway 16 to Elkins. It is still misty, gray from horizon to horizon. The only leaves left are on the oaks. We can see the lay of the land, the architecture of the trees, uncovered fences, cows in pastures, red and green and brown fields, barns and silos. We pass the Victory Free Will Baptist Church, Guernseys and Herefords, a field of Appaloosas, their black spots showing on their wet hides.

Near here the West Fork of the White meets the middle fork at the bottom of Lake Sequoyah. "The first dam on the lake is at Sequoyah," the Trout Fisherman says. Later we will learn that isn't so.

We go from 71 to 265 to 68 east, past Sonora, and onto Highway 16 toward Elkins. Between Tuttle and Elkins we get our first glimpse of the river before the dams.

Beautiful country. We drive past apple and peach orchards and vineyards with their black configurations set like Chinese characters against the tilled soil.

Near here, in Madison County, up around Red Star, a hundred little gaps and rises and valleys are the last hideouts of the hippies, the ones that went back to the land to stay.

Everything in the Ozarks is very simple still. Even pollution doesn't seem to have made great inroads into the beauty. Still, I remember when I first moved here, in 1979, and the scientist Anderson Nettleship, now deceased, would proclaim to me about acid rain falling on our forests from smokestacks thousands of miles away. I felt helpless in the face of that but Dr. Nettleship did not. He protested it loudly all his life, in person and in many letters to the Powers That Be.

Another thing he used to lecture me about was the sheer

idiocy of romantic love. "Childbirth, of course," he would begin, "is the true manifestation of the creative urge. But that is another matter." The Trout Fisherman and I knew Dr. Nettleship and loved to talk with him. If he had still been manifest he would have made a wonderful companion on this trip.

9:50: At Tuttle we get our first view of the river above the dams. Here the river is at its widest, sixty to a hundred feet. This is the river before it starts being fucked up. Wide green flood plains, bottomland as it's called in the hills, the watershed, what the river drains. Near Brashears we pass a house with white ceramic chickens and a red wagon beside a well. Perfect and right.

Near Combs there are white cattle against green and red fields. In the background a stand of white birch trees against a gray sky. A patch of sunlight beginning to show in the east.

I have been in this country this time of year when it is so golden and orange and transformed by sunlight that you can barely hold the car on the road. Black trees, orange leaves, blue skies, green moss, still green pastures, the rise and fall of a thousand hills, mountains in the distance. Dazzling. But it is proper that today is all gray drizzle and black trees and gray water pouring over white rocks. This is "water poetry time," as the Trout Fisherman calls it. Water falling from the sky, and all around, and underneath where the great aquifers stretch all the way to Alaska.

A day for mist and rain and water. I am feeling very chic in my hand-me-down raincoat, wondering if my boots will fit over my heavy wool socks. (We each have a pair of fine new socks, a gift from the Tentkeeper when we went by yesterday to pick up the tent.)

The Trout Fisherman hands me a cookie. He is always feeding me. He thinks I don't pay enough attention to myself.

*   *   *

11:00: We stopped at Fleming Creek to watch a flock of mallards on the water. The bridge over the creek is so old and rickety it's a wonder it held our Isuzu. We walked out across the rocks and stood in the middle of the creekbed watching cars go by, watching the sagging timbers of the supports sway and hold.

"What's keeping it up?" I asked.

"Acts of faith," the Trout Fisherman replied. "I hope it doesn't fall while we're watching." The Designated Driver had wandered off into the underbrush looking for photographs. We stood in the water admiring the sawdust blowing off the top of a huge sawdust mountain beside a sawmill. High hills all around with green pastures, ducks and cows and woodpeckers. Pollution seems so harmless when there isn't much of it.

11:30: We stopped again at St. Paul. Sugar Tree Mountain is visible from here, rising up so high and covered with a crown of mist. We went on, past Slow Tom Hollow and Hawkins Hollow Creek, past Dutton and on to Pettigrew. We had grown quiet, getting near our destination.

11:45: Four miles from Boston, at No Name Knob after Pettigrew. The river is getting very small, lost below its rocky red clay banks. The Designated Driver is driving. The Trout Fisherman is making up water poetry. I am almost asleep and wake just as we go up a hill past a mailbox marked *Love* and there is the Boston, Arkansas, post office, deserted on the crest of a hill. We stop the Isuzu and get out and take photographs. A book called *Married Sexual Happiness* is lying facedown on a box inside the deserted post office. The Trout Fisherman picks it up and smiles at me. The Trout Fisherman and I are always talking about getting married but we never do. We are both too gun-shy and selfish and set in our ways to make promises.

"Let's look for markers," the Designated Driver says and

the three of us leave the post office and start down the hill toward the ravine.

12:40: The Designated Driver and I walked down to where a geodesic survey marker stood up in the blackened leafless briers. The marker was about twenty feet below the shoulder of the road. *WH* it said in large block letters.

"White River," I announced. "This is it." Dave climbed down another thirty feet and found a second marker on a steeper incline above a gully where water runs in torrents in the spring. I had visions of the ridge covered with snow and the sun of early March melting the snow and sending it in rushes to fill the trough. "Oh, yes," I said. "This is surely it." It was all very mystical and cold and wonderful. What had started out as a lark, a created adventure for a magazine article, had turned into a mystery with deserted ridges on gray November days and a lost post office crowning the ridge exactly where it should be. The Designated Driver stood at the edge of the ravine holding his camera. I was above him imagining I was standing upon an aquifer, loving (more than ever) this craziness called Arkansas, a place where men are still free, in the old sense of the word, meaning some of them at least still create and live out their own destinies. Until recently there was a usury law in effect here. No human slavery in Arkansas, no licenses to steal.

The Designated Driver and I kept looking at each other. We weren't satisfied yet. The Trout Fisherman came back across the road and announced that the water came from higher up and we would have to climb. We crossed the road and followed a leaf-covered ridge that curved along the side of the hill below the post office. We could hear water, a steady drip and gurgle about a hundred yards back. Following it we came to a waterfall and twenty feet above that another one.

"Let's hike," the Trout Fisherman said. "Let's do some climbing."

"Let's go to the truck first and get some dry socks," I said. "We might be gone for a while."

"Let's talk to those folks across the road," the Designated Driver added. We left the waterfall and went back to the truck. A red Buick was coming down the hill from the post office. The driver was kind enough to stop and answer our questions. "You need to talk to Mrs. Hunter," she said. "She knows everything around here."

"Is that her house across the road?" the Trout Fisherman asked.

"Right there," the woman answered. "Just knock on the door. She'll be glad to talk to you."

Maybe Mrs. Irene Hunter is just the friendliest and most trusting person in the world. Or maybe it was the pair of long white socks the Trout Fisherman was holding in his hand when he knocked on her door. One way or the other she came right out and offered to help.

The driver of the Buick was right. Mrs. Hunter did know everything. In the first place she had been a forest ranger until her retirement several years ago. In the second place her nephew owns the land that holds the spring we were seeking. She went back inside for a coat and returned and got into the truck. She pointed out directions with beautiful sweeps of her hand. "Yes, four rivers rise on this little knob. The White runs to the north, the War Eagle to the west, the Kings to the east, and the Mulberry to the south." We were enchanted. She was a lovely graceful woman, widowed five years but not the kind of person who gives in to grief. Her children grown and her husband dead, she keeps on living in her house, a comfortable-looking white wooden dwelling across from the deserted post office.

With Mrs. Hunter giving directions, we drove past the post office and up a red dirt road to the crest of the rise. Tall yellow grasses bent beneath the rain. We were all very excited, we were on a great quest and had found the mythical wise woman who would show us the way. We drove through the high yellow grasses and got out and marched along to a small clear pond with a black tree growing up in the middle. "Right there," she said. "The spring starts underneath that tree." We walked out onto a narrow dam and stood trans-fixed. The dead tree stood up in the water like a symbol. It must have been a proud oak or maple before the first dam on the White River killed it and left its skeleton for a statue to mark the place.

We stood in the cold light rain and took photographs and whispered about the source of water. Not far away, in Eureka Springs, Arkansas, there is a spring whose waters are part of an aquifer that has its beginnings in Alaska.

Below the small dam the water continues down the ravine in waterfalls and comes to the place where we had left our footprints an hour before. Then on down and along its watercourse to where it meets up with the West Fork. Between here and there a thousand million trickles make music and run past the Designated Driver's dome and on to Fayetteville. Then the river doubles back and falls all the way down the state of Arkansas to meet the Mississippi across from Rosedale, where the Famous Writer's father was born, at the beginning of this century, when men still knew rivers and shared and used that knowledge.

We got back to Dave's house in the afternoon and made a fire and heated up the Wok Stew and started talking. It was the best of conversation, about night and the size of the universe and black holes and what fish do in the winter and fish the Trout Fisherman had caught and photographs the Designated Driver had taken and books we all would write and plays we would put on and movies we could film if they would only give us the chance. About the death of rock and roll and the secrets of DNA and how people lived a long time ago and the houses they built and who invented the hearth and what the hearth means and whether the world will end in fire or ice and if we will get what we want out of life in the meantime.

We talked about babies in the womb and ecstasy and

poetry and songwriting and how to catch trout and how to print photographs that will last forever and how the Cajuns put their photographs in enamel on their graves and Leonardo da Vinci and Walter Anderson and Ginny Stanford and the upcoming wedding of Kathleen Whitehead who started wearing her wedding band the day her fiancé bought it. We talked about the hard job of being a young man in the modern world. About how hard it is to figure out what to do for a living and how hard it is to come up to everyone's expectations and how young women are so strong nowadays that a man has to really get cracking to catch and hold a good one. About how to be a man and who to emulate and what to learn and what to know. "You got to know when to hold 'em," as Kenny Rogers sings. "Know when to fold 'em. Know when to walk away. Know when to run."

Finally, we threw the last log on the fire, finished off the brandy, and went to bed listening to the river and the dry branches in the November trees. "Goodnight," I called out. "I love you both. Thanks for taking me." "We love you too," they called back.

Love, it said on the mailbox. What else does a Famous Writer want from a magazine assignment?

ℂℙ

THERE WAS a wonderful piece in the *New Yorker* in which the writer explains the Zeitgeist, the way ideas or fads or states of mind spread throughout a culture with the speed of light. All of a sudden everyone has a crew cut or marches on Washington or decides to be very very thin or decides to give up on being very very thin.

I have always been a bellwether of such fads. I was one of the first women in New Orleans to go out running in Audubon Park. I was one of the first ones to quit. Anyone who has ever known me will attest that I have been at the cutting edge of every diet and exercise fad in the United States. All this time I have weighed exactly the same. Except for times when I was too busy to think about my body, during which times, for some mysterious reason, I would become quite thin.

At the moment I have given it all up. As an adult in a world where eating disorders have become a real problem and a menace, I think it is my place to stop acting like a neurotic teenager and set an example of harmony and balance. So all I am doing now is walking a few miles a day and eating anything I want except sugar. Also, I have vowed never to eat another salad unless I really want it and I am having an easy time keeping that promise to myself.

Here is the good news. It is eight weeks later and I haven't gotten fat. I've been eating when I was hungry and nothing bad has happened. Amazing. It is like some terrible spell has been broken. Also I quit weighing myself. I have thrown those damn scales away for good. A steel box with a set of revolving numbers is not going to have the power to ruin or make my day. What a metaphor the body-weight obsession of our century makes. Scales and surrogate mothers and nuclear warheads and mean-spirited people being delighted that young men are dying of Acquired Immune Deficiency Syndrome. I've got about thirty more years to live here, in this culture, with this madness. I may not escape all of it, but I am running as hard as I can. I'm going to begin by learning to love my own little soft round useful hungry healthy body.

FOR A LONG TIME I have wanted to set something straight in the world. There are many people who read my books and decide that I am a feminist. I believe they base this assumption on the stories that deal with an intense sibling rivalry between a little redheaded girl named Rhoda and her brother, Dudley, poorly disguised versions of my brother Dooley and myself. This real-life Dooley is three and a half years older than I am and he was always the pet. My mother liked him best and my father liked him best and my paternal grandmother liked him best. He was always getting his Eagle Scout badge or going to the Junior Olympics or stoking the furnace or carrying out the garbage or being brave when he put out his eye and playing championship golf and football and basketball and track anyway. He went on to father ten children and become a big-game hunter with a reputation for courage in the face of danger and so forth and so on. My problems with him, however, had nothing to do with male and female roles. It was pure sibling rivalry, a bitter battle for the minds and hearts of our parents.

On top of everything else he has done to me he goes on loving me more than I love him, as a Big Brother should. I know, for example, that if I was in a hospital with some terrible cancer and no one else would do it, he would shoot me if I asked him to. He would kill or die for me and that brings me to the real subject of this essay. I like men because they protect me. All my life they have protected me and I believe they will go on doing it as long as I love them in return.

I like men. I like the way they look at themselves in mirrors, quickly, with a sort of sleight-of-hand pride.

I have two brothers and nine male first cousins and three sons and four uncles and a grandson and three ex-husbands. All of them are good-looking and all of them like themselves. Women like them and I like them and they like themselves. They had good mothers. It takes a good mother to make a good man. It takes a woman loving a man to death when he is small to turn him into a man who will kill or die for the women he loves.

I suppose I should modify my statement and say that I like good-looking men who will kill or die for me.

"I don't know what you women expect of us," a philosopher and ex–Vanderbilt football player once said to me. "Goddammit, you expect us to be gentlemen twenty-four hours a day and ready to kill at a moment's notice."

"Yes," I answered. "That is what we have always expected."

It is what we have expected. Down through the countless ages of human life, women have held the babies in their arms while men fought for them. This is not some sort of joke or cartoon. This is the reality of who we are and where we came from. All our modern associations with each other come from that long, indelible history. Once, when my first grandchild was about three months old, I went with his mother and father on a long car trip from New Orleans, Louisiana, to Austin, Texas. I sat in the back of my daughter-in-law's old black Buick pretending I was the grandmother in a Flannery O'Connor short story, wishing I was wearing a hat. I was holding the baby. My son was driving and my daughter-in-law was riding shotgun. We talked about men and women and babies all the way to Texas. It was our plan to figure things out before we got to Austin so the two of them could lead a long and happy life and make a perfect home for the little boy I was holding in my arms. I have forgotten all the things we said or the points we made and argued about and discussed. I remember that we gave up after two hundred miles and decided it was a subject that did not reveal its secrets.

But this is boring grandmother talk and men want me to tell them how beautiful they are and how much we like the way their shoulders grow so wide and their arms so long and how we love their voices to be deep and how we like them to laugh at us and pretend we are dumber than they are. Maybe men don't like that anymore. I know it was out of style for a while. I'm not talking about dumb, like in dumb blondes with small intelligence quotients. I mean dumb, like in let's pretend, just for this evening, or until I get you to say you love me, that maybe you are a bit better informed, able to reach logical conclusions faster, and certainly you can add and subtract better than I can. Otherwise why are you doing that boring income-tax return while I polish my fingernails.

There is another game that I play with my male cousins. It is called I look like a woman and wear this skirt and these high-heeled shoes and so forth but you knew me when and you know that you and I can drink all these bohoes under the table because we are kin to each other and equal where it really matters, in the endless childhood of our shared past.

I love pride in a man. I don't care if it inconveniences me because I can't push a proud man around or make him do what I want him to do or even quit smoking until he gets damn good and ready. I like to see a man square his shoulders and prepare to take a stand. There were all those fifty million years around those campfires after the sun went down and the big cats came out. Maybe power to confront that night is what I'm seeing when I watch a man draw himself up to his full height and tell me no.

Most of my close friends are men. I like women but they hold no surprises for me. I know the good things about women and the bad things about them and as long as they are strong and brave and don't blame things on other people or act like they're sick I like them as much as I do men. Still, the range of possibilities is all within my scope. Not so with men. Men are a mystery to me. I once loved a man who liked to fish. He could stand so still waiting for a fish to bite. It amazed me to watch him fish. I could not understand the patience he gave to it or his delight in the catch or the deep incomprehensible satisfaction it gave him. I think he had been fishing a long time. Maybe for fifty million years.

I loved another man who liked to look at stars through a telescope. He would spend hours on the porch in the dark looking at stars without ever becoming frightened of death and needing to come inside. I would watch him and wonder what he was seeing that I would never see if I looked through a telescope. When I look at the rings of Saturn or the moons of Jupiter all I think about is whether or not we will have to go there to live and if so, how will we keep the children warm.

But I am an old-fashioned woman. I don't want to be a man. I don't want to have broad shoulders or big arms or be the one to go out and fight the big cats or the invading Huns or whatever threatens us next. I want to go on living side by side with men and running my hands up and down the muscles of their arms and worrying about them and talking about them behind their backs to other women.

I can say all that and still know that women are actually wiser than men because we are more intuitive and, of course, much as I hate to bring this up, we do bring them into the world.

I like the clothes men wear. Once I loved a man so much I made him a white cotton shirt with my own hands. I loved another one so much I wrote three books to get his attention. There is an old gorgeous man living right here in Jackson, Mississippi, that I have been loving and fighting with and showing off for since I was born fifty-one years ago. My mother's only husband. My father and I have almost stopped arguing now that he is seventy-seven and I am fifty-one. This is a cause of great concern to a friend of mine who is still arguing morning, night, and noon with his twenty-year-old daughter. "You mean I have to wait until I am seventy-seven years old to get Anna Katherine to be friends with me?" He shook his big intelligent head. "I have known thousands of people in my lifetime and I have always been able to talk sensibly with any of them except for my daughter. Why is that? How can that be?"

"Back to the old campfires," I tell him. "If you didn't argue and fight with her you might like her too much."

"But it's nineteen eighty-six. It's the modern world."

"So they tell me." I reach out and run my hand up and down his arm, not forgetting to give a few pats to the gorgeous breadth of his shoulders. "You can take it," I tell him. "You're tough."

He drew himself up to his full height and invited me to go out to dinner at a place called the Sundancer.

Once, there was an autograph party for one of my books in a bookstore in the same shopping center as the Sundancer and when the book signing in the store was over my baby brother invited everyone in the store to have dinner on him at the Sundancer. He took a box of fifty books with him and sold them at the bar while we ate dinner.

Surrounded by men like that I would have to be crazy not to love men. Women who really love men may have to spend a certain amount of time running their hands up and down someone's arms, but they are almost never crazy.

♈

IN 1985 I was asked to give the Baccalaureate address at the J. William Fulbright College of Arts and Sciences at the University of Arkansas. Wearing a long black gown and a mortarboard and my old handmade leather sandals from the Flying Possum on Dickson Street, I climbed the rickety stairs and faced an audience of friends and students and college professors. It seemed to be the most momentous occasion of my life but what I was feeling was not hubris. I gathered my courage to the sticking place and began. Here is what I said.

I am honored to be here. I want to thank the faculty for inviting me and all of you for allowing me to give you the last official lesson you will ever have at this college.

I want to tell you the best things I know before you leave here. Unfortunately, most of them are in the words of other people. All my life I have been a reader. Before I could actually read I used to pretend to read. And reading has colored and changed my life and made me different and made me rich.

Several times in my life I have been rich in money, had at my disposal more money than I could think of ways to spend, and each time I went out and deliberately got rid of the money. I got rid of the money because it is a bore and a terrible responsibility. A roof over my head, honest work to do, friends, books to read, a small income so I can work in peace. These are things that money can properly buy. Large sums of money that allow you at a distance to rule and order the lives of other people and demand their time and labor bring their own bad karma with them. And something worse. They bring fear.

A rich man is always afraid he will lose his money. At any moment the treasure he so desired may be stolen or taken from him and then where will he be?

I want to talk to you this morning about another kind of richness. A richness that is represented by and kept safe in and passed on by colleges and libraries, the repositories of the best ideas man has ever had. The poetry and philosophy and knowledge of the physical universe that thousands of minds over thousands of years have left here for your teachers to pass on to you.

The men and women who have taught you, for your sake, and for their own, and for the sake of all mankind, have been attempting piece by piece and bit by bit to give you some part of that incredible inheritance. If nothing else to awaken in you in a hunger for more of this sort of knowledge.

Do not go out into the world and read only newspapers and magazines and watch the unbelievably impoverished and hypnotic junk that is on television. Do not get your fiction and myth from movies and your philosophy and poetry from magazines. It is not only because I write books that I want you to read them. But because I don't want to live in a world where most of the people I pass on the street haven't had anything to think about all week but headlines in newspapers and the stuff that passes for entertainment on television. I have worked for television and magazines. I know how frightened and scattered the people are who make the stuff you are being bored and confused and brainwashed by.

Enough. I swore I wouldn't preach to you. I swore I wouldn't act like you were on your way to the North Pole and I was the last agent at the last commissary passing out supplies for the trip and that if I forgot to give you anything you couldn't get it where you are going.

If you leave here and never read real books anymore, hard books, the kind that can't be read while watching television, then you will be going somewhere where the things I want to give you aren't available.

I spent several weeks walking around my house trying to write this speech. I was getting a lot of advice from all around town and on the phone from California and New York and Jackson, Mississippi.

My mother called at least three times to beg me not to sound like an agnostic. My editor kept worrying that I would talk to you about freedom and forget to say that freedom entails responsibility. A young friend who works for Skyways said she thought maybe it would be better if I didn't write it down but just got up and talked.

My lawyer said he thought I should talk to you about kissing since that is probably the only thing you haven't already been lectured to about and since it might be the most honest and meaningful thing most of you would be doing from now on.

That was a strange and complicated thing to say, and not entirely cynical. My own best idea was to walk up to the microphone and tell you the only role I ever wanted was to be the mother in the musical *Hair* who climbs up on the stage clutching her pocketbook and says, "Now, kids, do whatever you want to do, be whatever you want to be, as long as you don't hurt anybody. And, remember, I am your friend."

By last Saturday I was getting frantic. I never have trouble writing anything. Writing is as natural to me as talking. This is the most trouble I have gone to in years to write something. Finally, I went out and walked around the mountain and decided what to do. I decided to tell you the best things I know. They were written by other men and women. I found them inside the covers of books that were hard to read. I found them and learned them and they represent the true riches of my life.

These things came from books that were the products of long hours and days of thought and editing, visions and revisions, the best parts of the best minds that have ever lived on earth, the essence, your real and true inheritance, that no one can cheat you out of, or steal from you or take from you in any way. As long as there are colleges and libraries and free men this inheritance will be waiting for you and you can come and get some of it whenever you get tired of kissing.

Here are some samples of what is waiting. This is from the first volume of the autobiography of Bertrand Russell. From the prologue, called "What I Have Lived For."

Three passions, simple but ungovernably strong, have ruled my life. The longing for love, the search for wisdom and unbearable pity for the suffering of mankind. These passions, like great winds, have blown me hither and thither in a wayward course, over a deep ocean of anguish, reaching to the very verge of despair.

I have sought love, first, because it brings ecstasy, ecstasy so great that I would often have sacrificed all the rest of my life for a few hours of this joy. I have sought it next, because it relieves loneliness, the terrible loneliness in which one shivering consciousness looks over the rim of the world into the cold unfathomable lifeless abyss. I have sought it finally, because in the union of love I have seen, in mystic miniature, the prefiguring vision of the heaven that saints and poets have imagined. This is what I have sought, and though it might seem too good for human life, this is what, at last, I have found.

With equal passion I have sought knowledge. I have wished to understand the hearts of men. I have wished to know why the stars shine. And I have tried to apprehend the Pythagorean power by which number holds sway above the flux. A little of this, but not much, I have achieved.

Love and knowledge, as far as they were possible, led upwards towards the heavens, but always pity brought me back to earth. Echoes of cries of pain reverberate in my heart. Children in famine, victims tortured by oppressors, helpless old people a hated burden to their sons, and the whole world of loneliness, poverty and pain make a mockery of what human life should be. I long to alleviate the evil but I cannot and I too suffer.

This has been my life. I have found it worth living, and would gladly live it again if the chance were offered me.

Try reading that on a rainy day when you are lonely or a long way from home.

And now I'm going to read you what is perhaps my single favorite piece of writing. It is from *The Once and Future King,* by T. H. White.

"The best thing for being sad," replied Merlin, beginning to puff and blow, "is to learn something. That is the only thing that never fails. You may grow old and trembling in your anatomies, you may lie awake at night listening to the disorder of your veins, you may miss your only love, you may see the world about you devastated by evil lunatics, or know your honor trampled in the sewers of baser minds. There is only one thing for it then, to learn. Learn why the world wags and what wags it. That is the only thing which the MIND can never exhaust, never alienate, never be tortured by, never fear or distrust, and never dream of regretting. Learning is the thing for you. Look at what a lot of things there are to learn — pure science, the only purity there is. You can learn astronomy in a lifetime, natural history in three, literature in six. And then, after you have exhausted a milliard lifetimes in biology and medicine and theocriticism and geography and history and economics — why, then you can start to make a cartwheel out of the appropriate wood, or spend fifty years learning to begin to learn to beat your adversary at fencing. After that you can start again on mathematics, until it is time to learn to plough."

"Apart from all those things," said the Wart. "What do you suggest for me just now?"

I raised my children with that quotation for advice. It's what I did instead of feel sorry for them. *The Once and Future King.* It took T. H. White twenty-five years to write that book.

Here is a piece of your inheritance that was written thousands of years ago by a man named Heraclitus. "All men are deceived by the appearances of things, even Homer himself, who was the wisest man in Greece; for he was deceived by boys catching lice; they said to him, 'What we have caught we have left behind, but what has escaped us we bring with us.' "

Lastly, I would like to read you two lines from Eudora Welty's wonderful, outrageous book, *The Robber Bridegroom*. It takes place on the Natchez Trace and concerns a number of characters, including the infamous bandits, Little Harp and Big Harp. "Little Harp hated to see anything penned up. Anything he saw penned up he would turn loose, himself included." And so, in the spirit of Little Harp, I turn you loose to do anything you want to do and be anything you want to be, as long as you don't hurt anybody, and promise to read some books. Go in peace then, and remember, I am your friend.

Further
Reflections

In Praise of the Young Man

*H*E WAS twenty-six and I was forty-four. He took me down rivers in canoes and built fires in the woods for me and taught me not to be afraid. I followed him places I had always dreamed of going. When I was a child, my father and my brothers would strike out for the woods leaving me behind. This time I was not left behind. I was the *cause* of the expeditions. I was the girl sitting on the floor of the canoe reading fashion magazines while my beautiful lover guided the canoe over treacherous waters. Could I have resisted such seduction? Could anyone have resisted it?

I lost ten pounds the first month I knew him. I lost twenty years. At a time when most women my age are worrying about menopause I thought I was *pregnant* when I stopped menstruating. That was completely impossible since I had had a tubal ligation years before; still, the idea was exciting and later I wrote a novel out of the fantasy and made a lot of money from it.

He taught me to shoot pool. He bought me a baseball shirt with blue sleeves. He made love to me one afternoon in the back seat of a car. I had never made love in an automobile. I thought it was hilarious. I thought it was the freest and funniest thing I had ever done. Beside a lake, in a remote part of a national park, I took off my underpants and made love in the back seat of a car.

He taught me to sing. He taught me that if you know the words you won't forget the tune. He taught me to sing, "Mamas, Don't Let Your Babies Grow Up to Be Cowboys." He would let me sing it over and over again when we went on car trips.

He sang to me. He would take his guitar out of his guitar case and sit on my piano bench tuning it for a long time before he began to sing. He would sing songs he was composing and songs he was practicing and finally, because he knew I was waiting for it, he would sing, "Dance with Me, I Want to Be Your Partner."

It was the first song he had ever sung to me. On the day we met, he played it for me on a balcony at sundown. An hour later, when the world was dark, he asked me to marry him. This is the way to win a woman. This is the way a woman wants to fall in love.

He did dance with me. He danced with me in my living room and in nightclubs and on sidewalks at dark in distant cities. He danced with me as if I were an extension of his own body and his joy in dancing made me graceful.

When I met him I had just moved to a small town in the Ozark mountains. One reason I had moved there was to be near the woods. I longed for woods, for rivers, and wilderness. After I met the young man, he became my guide. He had always lived in the area and knew the rivers and woods like he knew sun and rain.

He would drop anything to go camping. It would pour down rain for several days, and he would turn to me and say, "This rain is going to fill up all the rivers. We should go down one while we can. When they're full the sissies won't be in the way." Then we would throw a change of clothes into a plastic bag, grab the tent, and be out the door. One morning we set off down the Buffalo River when the water was two feet above the bridges. I don't know how we talked the canoe shop into renting us a canoe, except the owner knew the young man and trusted him not to get us killed.

He could guide a canoe down a river without seeming to move a muscle. He had Indian blood and he believed it made the earth his friend. His old Cherokee grandfather had taught him to fish and hunt and live in the woods. He didn't like equipment. A cigarette lighter and a sack of crackers and cheese was all he needed to enter the woods and live for days.

What did we talk about during those long days and nights when we were alone on rivers and riverbanks and in woods? I think we talked about ourselves, telling the stories of our lives, laughing about what people were saying about us behind our backs. We thought it was hilarious that people thought I was old and he was young. We were not old or young to each other. We were in love and had been since the day we met.

Perhaps we only imagined that people were talking about us *behind our backs*. The people who were interested in us were over at my house talking *to us* and listening to us talk about ourselves. A passionate love affair is a strange attractor. People cannot stay away from happiness and joy. Healthy people are swept up by love, which is why so much time and energy is happily spent on weddings.

A famous scientist in town became the mentor of our love affair. He was at least seventy years old and had degrees from Oxford, England and Edinborough, Scotland. He loved to be around the young man and me. He would sit in my living room and watch us interact and later he would talk to me about it. Once, when I said I thought I should end the relationship and force the young man to find a woman his own age, the scientist said to me, "Why are women always thinking they can tell men what to want? All men don't have to want the same things. Men are as complicated as women are, although women don't want to believe that's true. Why do you keep questioning and probing this happiness you have? Why can't you just be content with it?"

"They aren't all as complicated as women," I replied.

"The good ones are," he answered. "The only ones you would be interested in knowing. The ones who write songs about you."

The young man had been writing a song about me. He had taken the central premise of a book I had written and turned it into a beautiful, small lyric. The song was plaintive, simple, clean. It said the thing he never said to me in words. I love you and I will lose you because this is a land of dreams.

What were people saying about us? Young artists and writers around town were basically tolerant. The older male writers either wanted to think it was a joke or talk me out of it. The women mostly understood or else thought it was good revenge on older men who go out with younger women. I supposed their reactions were insights into their own needs and personalities. To tell the truth I didn't give a damn what any of them thought.

A journalist in my town says I used to wear the young man like a bangle on a bracelet. I did occasionally like to take him around people my own age and watch him charm them. He was a charming man, intelligent and well-read, with a deep feeling of good-will toward other people.

There are deeper truths to what went on between us. On the day I met the young man, I had just learned that my daughter-in-law was carrying my oldest grandchild. I was in ecstasy at this news. Perhaps I fell in love with the young man to be part of all that fecundity and life. I had these two great happinesses at the same time.

I would wake from sleep during those months in a state of bliss. Every shaft of light seemed intense and beautiful. The taste and feel of water was almost unbearable in its beauty, clarity, purity. Every tree and flower and change of weather seemed charged with meaning and with purpose.

There were darker truths to the relationship. There were things about his life that I could never understand or accept. There were dark, controlling parts of my personality that surprised and wounded him. I was full of old selfishness, anxieties, and fears. He was full of old resentments. When we would try to live together these elements would ignite and burn.

* * *

My oldest son was enraged by the affair. He thought I should be content to be a grandmother. By the time he met the young man, my grandchild had been born and my son thought I should follow in my mother's footsteps and devote my life to my progeny. It was of no interest to my son that I had just published a book to great critical acclaim and had an exciting career and a life of my own. All he knew was that I was breaking the patterns of the past. It was many years before he forgave me for this, if he has forgiven me, and I'm not sure he has.

The young man's family was probably equally unhappy about the love affair, but I never knew the details of that. If they spoke to him about it, he never told me what they said. As much as we could we stayed away from both our families. We tried to protect each other from their intrusions and I think we did a good job of that. Once, after we had known each other for many years, I took the young man to Jackson, Mississippi to meet my parents. They called me up two nights later. They were eighty-two at the time. I was fifty-seven. "That won't do," my father said, when he got me on the phone. "This business with the young man has got to stop."

My mother got on the other phone. "You will have to get rid of him," she added. "I'm sure your children are embarrassed to death by this."

"Nothing I could do to them could be as bad as the things they have done to me," I answered, in the nasty tone I reserve for talking to my mother. "I am fifty-seven years old, Mother. I am hanging up."

The young man and I were always hanging up on the world. When we were together nothing the outside world did seemed to be able to harm what went on between us. We made each other happy and we made each other laugh and we made each other strong. When we were together love was its own protection, a barrier against reality.

* * *

Of course it had to end. I always knew it had to end. I told him in the beginning I would be his girl until I was fifty years old. I was almost sixty when it finally really ended. We had broken up and made up many times during those years but always without rancor or ill-will. The truth was we couldn't stay away from each other. We had created a paradise when we first met and when we were apart we would long to have it back. He would call me or I would call him and within an hour we would be in bed. We would lie in each other's arms and tell the story of how we met and fell in love and told the world to go to hell. We shared a fabulous story of who we had been together, of what we had dared and what we had created.

I have been in psychotherapy for many years. I know that the young man was a surrogate for my sons who had grown up and gone off to have lives of their own. I know that for him I was the mother all men dream of having. The mother who is their sole property. The mother who adores them without question. I know these psychological realities were the ground for our disagreements and the reason the relationship could never last. I knew this while it was going on but it did not change a thing.

Love is a goddess. It is the honey to end all honeys. No one turns down Aphrodite when she comes to call. The old Greeks knew how to create a metaphor. The goddess of love with her satisfied, enigmatic smile. Her little son beside her with his quiver of arrows. He lifts his bow, he takes aim, he shoots, and a man or woman falls into a spell from which there is no escape.

Perhaps I loved him because he was different from other men I had known. He never turned on a television set. He was a small-town boy and read the local newspaper and liked knowing what was going on in the place where he lived. He didn't care what was happening in New York City or Washington, D.C. He wanted to know who was running for sheriff and what was on at the movies and who won the high school football games.

I learned from him to love the place where we were, at that moment, on any given day. I had moved around a great deal as a child, and I had never learned to give my allegiance to a place.

He taught me love. Not just romantic love, and God knows it was romantic, but love of place. He would drive me around and show me places that he loved. An old oak tree that had been split in two by lightning half a century before. Two trees grew from the split trunk with a view of the distant mountains in the space between them.

He took me to the Confederate cemetery on a fall day with the maple trees golden above the graves. A few weeks later, he took me back to see the golden carpet the leaves had become. He never told me where we were going on these expeditions. We would just get into the car, and he would turn on the radio and drive slowly and carefully to something he wanted me to see. He took me out in the country to see his childhood swimming holes. He took me to see the place where his mother taught him to swim. He was very sentimental about that small, weed-bordered lake. He always spoke of his mother with love and praise and because of that I knew I was safe to believe he loved me. A man who loves his mother can love other women. A man who resents his mother will sooner or later resent you if he loves you.

None of that had much to do with young and old. Love is liking to be with another person, having a good time in their presence, thinking you are good and valuable when you are with them.

I remember the first time he saw my forty-four year old body in a bathing suit. He was taking me swimming in a beautiful clear lake formed by the dammed-up waters of the

White River. As usual he did not tell me where we were going. We took bathing suits and a lunch and got in the car and started driving. We drove for more than an hour, going north and west from home, going deep into the Ozark Mountains. We turned finally into a park and drove around and up to an overhang and parked the car and got out and started walking.

We walked down wide granite steps that had once been the top of a mountain. I have always loved to swim in lakes and rivers. I learned to swim in a bayou in the Mississippi Delta, and I love the taste and feel of brown river water. We changed into our bathing suits in a grove of shrub trees. "This is the body of a forty-four year old woman in a bathing suit," I said. "What do you think?"

"I think you look wonderful," he said. "Hold my hand."

Then we walked down the granite steps to the water, and he watched as I slid into the lake and started swimming. No man giving a woman diamonds ever had more pleasure or self-assurance in their gifts than he did in giving me that blessed lake.

Am I romanticizing all of this? Perhaps. I have had two great love affairs in my life. I don't think either of them need romanticizing.

I treasure the memory of that love affair, and I am always glad it happened. It made me understand my sons. It reminded me, at a time when many women are leaving such things behind, what passion is and does and causes, how it takes over and calls the shots and creates its own reality. It is a memory "never to be bartered against the hungry days."

How to have a small dinner party:

I never cook anything, and I don't like to cook things or clean up the mess it makes. I do, however, know how to cook several things. I know how to cook rare roast beef. You go to the grocery store and buy the most expensive rump roast you can find. You take it out of the paper and rinse it off and then put it in an old black skillet and cook it at 325 degrees Fahrenheit for twenty minutes per pound. Don't drink martinis while you are doing this or you will forget to take it out, and then you will have brisket instead of rare roast beef. While it is cooking, make some grits and stir in a pound of Kraft Extra Sharp Cheddar Cheese and half a stick of butter. Put this in a casserole, and cook it in a different oven at 350 degrees Fahrenheit for about twenty or thirty minutes. Cut up some lettuce and tomatoes if they are in season but not in the winter when you have to get those little sour hothouse tomatoes that are probably poison. Set the table. Use all the good silver and light some candles. Put some Bach on the stereo. Call the drugstore and tell them to send out the Sunday *New York Times* and a quart of chocolate ice cream in case no one wants any rare roast beef.

Make some coffee. Bon Appetit!

Ⴍ₽

[Supersonic flight, passage through the air at speed greater than the local velocity of sound. . . . The first supersonic passenger-carrying, commercial airplane, the Concorde, was built jointly by aircraft-manufacturing enterprises of the British and French governments. Traveling at Mach 2, or 1,200 miles an hour, it entered regular service on January 21, 1976.]

Encyclopedia Britannica

* * *

At the risk of bragging, I must begin this story with a piece of personal history. In 1984 I won the National Book Award for Fiction. In the light of this unexpected and dazzling event, I went to live in New York City for the winter. I rented a furnished apartment on the Upper East Side, certain I would soon be rich and famous and able to afford such luxuries. I spent the award money as though it would last forever. I have a strong imagination, but even I could not have imagined that all this would lead up to supersonic flight.

The year before, I had been on an elevator at the Algonquin Hotel with Eudora Welty, her friend Jane Petty, and the owner of the hotel. I was there to see Ms. Welty and Ms. Petty off on the *Queen Elizabeth* to visit Ms. Welty's European writing friends. As the elevator rose, the hotel owner was talking about her recent trip to London on the Concorde. "It was the single most luxurious thing I have ever done," she said. "We were there in three hours. No jet lag and the food was marvelous.

"Weren't you scared?" I asked.

"Of course not, Silly," she answered and fixed me with a haughty stare.

I had been in New York a month when my British publisher called and asked me to come to London to meet the British press and tour the building that houses Faber and Faber. Being published in England by Faber and Faber was another dream come true, and I accepted the invitation with alacrity. "Go on the Concorde," my agent advised. "It's a once in a lifetime experience." I thought it over. I remembered the elevator conversation and the hotel owner's haughty stare. I'll do it, I decided. Damn the torpedoes and all that.

A week later, on a beautiful clear Wednesday morning, I took a taxi to JFK and went into the elegant Concorde lounge to await the flight. I was dressed up in my best tweed jacket, my lucky yellow scarf, and a pair of high-heeled leather boots.

The flight was scheduled to leave at nine. We would be in London at six in the evening, a flight of three hours given the time difference.

The flight was announced, and I boarded the airplane and found myself sitting across the aisle from the president of Lloyd's of London, the company which insures the plane. Aside from us, there were only ten or eleven other passengers. We had the Concorde to ourselves.

It was a beautiful cabin. The plane was still relatively new, and the seats were twice as wide as they are now and covered with hand-tooled pale gray leather. Two stewardesses served coffee in china cups and gave us the first of many small gifts of candy and mementos. I have forgotten what they were except for one very small cut-glass battery-operated clock. But the thing that interested me most was a clock-size meter at the end of the aisle leading to the cockpit. "It records the speed," the president told me. "Keep your eye on it. You'll see it hit Mach 1 and then Mach 2."

The Concorde takes off vertically at six hundred miles an hour. When it has reached its altitude, which is high above commercial airline routes, it levels off, the nose cone realigns itself, and you can look out the windows and see the curvature of the earth. Then the real fun begins. Within fifteen minutes, the meter recorded that we had reached Mach 1. As that happened the plane seemed to stretch out, and I seemed to stretch out too. We were going faster than the speed of sound. In another fifteen minutes we passed Mach 2. The stewardesses moved up and down the aisle serving an elegant meal in five courses. The excitement was so thick you could taste it. I ate lunch, felt like an explorer, and chatted with the president of Lloyd's of London.

About two hours out from JFK, he asked if I had ever been to England. "No," I answered. "Although my ancestors all came from the British Isles."

"Then come along," he said. "I think you should go up to the cockpit."

A minute later, I was being ushered down the aisle and into the cockpit. Inside were the pilot, the co-pilot, and the first officer. They offered me a fourth seat across from the first officer. In front of me was a wide curving window. Out of it, I could see the British Isles just coming into view through the evening mist. We were breaking the Concorde record and arriving in London in less than three hours. "I can't tell you how much I appreciate your letting me come in here," I said. "I promise not to touch anything."

The pilot turned around in his seat and smiled at me. "Actually," he said, "it might be better if none of us touched anything."

I sat strapped into my seat, so thrilled it's a wonder I can remember any of this, as the computers landed the Concorde on the island of my genes. The Concorde now weighed two thirds less than when it took off. We had burned up the weight in fuel which is why this experience will soon be a thing of the past. I was lucky to have been there and to have thought I was rich enough to buy the ticket. The memory of that flight, of that moment when I went past my experience of myself, will be with me always. I was a golden Icarus who did not fall to earth but went gently gliding down.

℔

THERE ARE PEOPLE in the world who do not love the hot heat of summer. They are the same people who never read *The Bobbsey Twins in the Country*, who never had Fourth of July parades around their neighborhoods, whose brother never set off a whole package of firecrackers in a culvert and lived to tell the story. I love the heat. I know how to turn the air-conditioning down to sixty without a trace of guilt. It's survival of the fittest in the mortal world, and I come from a long line of men and women who knew how to fill a room with fans. Ceiling fans, rotating fans, tall fans that blew a steady breeze into my face when I was five feet tall. I was destined to grow up to be a woman who could turn the air-conditioner down and pay later. Best of all were hand-held fans, with which people of good will fanned each other. My six-foot-four inch grandfather used to fan people with his hat. I have a vivid memory of him standing on a country road fanning the man who was changing the tire on his Ford.

In the Deep South of my childhood we worked summer the way people in Minnesota work their frozen winters. We knew how to find shade, how to sleep away the hottest hours, how to kill flies and mosquitos, how to fish and barbecue, and use the heat to prove our mettle and our skills. We did not complain all the time about the heat. We moved the fans around the rooms to create breezes and watched the skies for rain and laid down on clean white bedspreads and read books.

I am always nostalgic during summer. Every summer brings memories of the ones that preceded it. Only yesterday I looked up and noticed the tulip vine was blooming beside my mailbox. Another year has passed. I had forgotten that scraggly vine produced those exotic, indescribably beautiful flowers.

Forty years ago this summer, I ran away and got married. In a borrowed Chevrolet, with an eighteen year old boy from Georgia, wearing a white dress with pearl buttons down the front, in a fever of curiosity, I got married. The boy and I bought a license and found a judge and promised to love each other until we died. Perhaps we do. Perhaps we will. It would never have happened in January.

One of my favorite things about summer is that the neighborhood children don't have to go to school. They have time to cut the yard, wash the windows, and accompany me on bicycle rides. They bring me up to date on the lyrics of Pearl Jam, the desperate politics surrounding election to the cheering squad and the dark side of the personalities of various high school and junior high school teachers. If you think adult life is fraught with peril, spend some time talking to people in the ninth grade.

Summer is always rich in children where I live. My grandchildren come to visit. Since I am fortunate in having married and bred at an early age, I am still sufficiently ambulatory to accommodate them when they wish to learn to ride bicycles and horses. This summer I am thinking of taking the thirteen year old out to a country road and teach him to drive. In honor of the summers long ago when my uncle let me drive trucks and farm equipment on my grandmother's farm. Also, in honor of Eudora Welty's great line, "Oren was eleven, a wonderful driver."

There are, of course, dark sides to summer. Lying in wait for the fine, fat arms and legs of the children are the bugs of summer, the flaw in paradise, the mistake that proves that if there is a God he is far from perfect, maybe even daft.

Who would make a tick? There is no conceivable, earthly use for a tick. A tick is not going to turn out to contain a cure for cancer. The tick is at the top of a list of reasons I might conceivably be glad when autumn comes. Ticks, wasps, flies, gnats, mosquitos, chiggers, maggots, fleas. To be balanced against butterflies, fireflies, dragonflies, honeysuckle, gardenias, robins, and the long days.

It is June 26th as I write this. We are past the zenith; we are on our way to winter. But first the real heat will set in. Drought will scare me into watering the trees; midday will be impossible; the interiors of automobiles will be too hot to touch. I will desire naps and wear shorts, even though fifty-nine year old women should probably be jailed for exhibiting their sun-damaged legs to the general view, or, even the uncritical eyes of their grandchildren.

I will lie down in the sun in the swing. I will add another layer to the subcutaneous damage to my skin. Who cares, I will think, drunk on the sun, what am I saving anything for? I will take a radio outside and play it on the back porch. I will watch a seven year old tirelessly hammering open hickory nuts for the squirrels to eat. I will feed the dog my son brought home to visit and promptly forgot.

"You want to go swimming?" the child will ask.

"Not till your food digests," I will answer. There is nothing I like better than passing on an old wives' tale to a child. "The chlorine will turn my hair green," I will add.

"Do you want it to?" she will answer. Seduced by her candor and her patient dedication to the welfare of the squirrels, I will rise from my lethargy and take her "to the pool." I wish I could take her on the great summer swims of my youth. Once I sneaked off with my cousin and went swimming in a cow pond. Once we sneaked off at night and swam in a borrow pit. Once I swam across a lake without a rowboat or a lifevest. If it was summer I was in the water. Only once in all that time did my hair actually turn green.

One never to be forgotten summer, I discovered a stash of magazines in my grandmother's attic. This was long ago when magazines routinely published continued stories. I was reading a continued novelette in *The Ladies Home Journal*. I had finished the first two installments and couldn't find the conclusion. I searched everywhere. I tore the attic apart. It was the story of a war wife whose young husband was shot down in the South Pacific. He crawled to safety in a cave but was reported missing in action. After three years, the wife has given up and is engaged to marry a naval officer. The young husband has been found and taken to a hospital in California. He has amnesia. All he can remember is the name of his wife. Angela Jane, he keeps repeating. A woman doctor who is in love with him is hot on the trail of a cure and an identification but she is conflicted. If he recovers his memory she will lose him. The young wife is picking out her blue dress for her second wedding. To be continued.

There were wasp nests in the attic. I was in constant danger as I searched for Part Three, which I never found. For years I asked magazine readers about that story but never found a soul who had read it or knew the ending. This tale makes a fine metaphor for summer. All that heat and drama, all those unresolved conflicts.

I have never wasted a summer, and I do not forget them. The heat imprints them on my brain. Winters all run together in my mind. I am wearing turtlenecks, building fires, turning up the thermostat, stamping my feet, locking doors, thinking, *it can't be dark yet. It's only six o'clock.*

In dreams of summer, I am always on a sleeping porch. Crickets and tree frogs are singing. It is the middle of the night. I am wide awake, scratching my chigger bites, thinking of wasp nests I will destroy with my broom, grateful another day has passed without my being bit by a tick carrying Rocky Mountain Spotted Fever, or, other, yet to be named and identified, diseases.

♎

I TURNED AROUND the other day and realized that summer was beginning to end. Late August, early September. The leaves will change and I will return to my books. Time to learn something. Time to study stars or atoms or time itself. Not that time exists. It is a construct, like language or belief. I intend to stop believing in it.

It has been a wonderful summer in the small university town where I live. Children came to visit and stayed for weeks. They had parades and sang to me and slept without moving through the long, hot nights. I slept near them, dreamless, timeless, caught in the wonder of their lives.

The days run away like wild horses over the hills, a poet wrote. It is that keen ecstasy which ends as summer ends. Time to open my closet and look things over. Move the dark clothes a little closer to the front. The black wool suit, the tweed jacket, the cocktail dress. Serious clothes. Not these cotton rags I pull on in the morning and dust the piano with on my way to bed at night.

There is a roadrunner living on my roof. He moves from the old hickory tree at the back of the house to the hickory in the front yard. This is a well-established pathway, having served generations of squirrels. We knew he was in the neighborhood. Several people had sighted him. I myself had seen him once, running beside the fence line in the direction of a wooded lot behind the houses. There has been a plethora of development in our town. The wildlife is doing the best it can under the circumstances.

It was my lifelong devotion to the theatre which led to my discovering that the roadrunner was living on the roof. An eight year old named Aurora and an eight year old named William were in the bathroom putting on clown makeup for a clown show. "Will you put up the tent cover so the show can go on in case of rain?" they asked me. "Of course," I answered. "Anything for art."

I went outside and began to drag a set of steel tent poles along the concrete porch. The noise startled the roadrunner from his afternoon nap, and he came tearing down across the roof. He spread his six-foot wingspan and flew the length of the porch, amazing my Bavarian daughter-in-law, who clutched the baby to her breast, believing she had seen an American eagle.

Where will the roadrunner go when the leaves turn yellow and carpet the concrete porch? Perhaps he will still find a way to live in my yard. Perhaps he will go back down the hill and live in one of the houses the greedy contractors are building in the flood plain that used to be a woods and a pasture. People in my neighborhood have watched with great interest as the new drainage ditches have failed to carry away the water when it rains. Surely no one will buy a house built on the lowest place in ten square miles. Perhaps they will. Human nature is very strange and hard to understand. Perhaps I will turn into a social critic now that fall is near. I will go down there and put up a sign that says, DON'T BUY A HOUSE HERE UNLESS YOU WANT WATER IN YOUR BASEMENT.

What *will* I do now that fall is coming? The children have all gone home. I can't hide behind my grandmother plumage any longer. I have a book to write. And one that will be published in September. That should be enough for anyone. But this time of year is insatiable. It wants vastness and adventure. Some hard use. Learn the Chinese language. Build a cathedral. Do yoga. Study Zen. Stop desiring anything. Anger, Greed, Pride, Fear, Desire, the five daughters of Maya, King of Darkness.

Hurry up, fall is always saying. Time is growing short. We don't have forever. Except I don't believe that. We have whatever we decide we have. Weeks spent with children pass like hours. Months spent writing a book seem like a weekend. Hours wondering what to do next seem like eons. Minutes waiting for someone are a well-known eternity. The main thing is to keep moving. Keep the pace that children keep. They rise from sleep and move into a day like sunlight. They burn until they fall. We are tilting on our axis. We are tilting further from the sun. Cold days and long nights are waiting. Exciting. I will shake out my sweaters and my high-heeled shoes, get airline tickets to northern cities, get a flu shot, get ready.

Enough of all this leaf, flower, bole. Enough of watching my neighbors water their lawns. Fall is the time for flowering. Gather in the sheaves, take the goods to market. I want to see Angel Corella dance at the American Ballet Theatre. I want to fly to London and see *Richard III*. I want to work all morning and exercise in the late afternoons and watch the senators fight on C-Span. In short, I am waking up, here at the end of summer, in the temperate climes, on the planet earth, in the only world there is.

I got out my Ansel Adams engagement calendar to see what I was doing this time last year. I had written on August 17, "You must change your life," Rainer Maria Rilke. Last fall

I was passionate about that. I stopped taking estrogen. Not for any medical or scientific reason but because I was tired of thinking about it. Since then I have learned that the estrogen I was taking is derived from mares who are deprived of water to make the urine stronger. It was bad karma to take that stuff and something in me knew it.

Also, I threw away my papers. I have no interest in some graduate student wasting her time going through the zeroxed copies of drafts of my books.

Next I suffered through the very last booksigning I will ever do. I am writing books to be read, not to be collected as souvenirs.

I won't have to look far to find other interesting junk to divest myself of this year. I have plenty of fears, dumb habits and insidious little prejudices I could pitch into the fires of autumn. The eight year old named William has a campground in his backyard with a ring of stones for building fires. Sometimes his parents let him cook his dinner there. The next time I see his smoke I will write down some stupid things I keep doing and take the paper over and burn it on his fire. On that day I will officially declare that summer is over.

A Southern Christmas

I WONDERED if I should begin this piece by saying, my brothers spent the morning with their wives and the afternoon with their mistresses. But that was later, after we were corrupted by prosperity. The Christmas I want to write about was long ago, in a time of innocence and war.

Christmases everywhere and in all times are fraught with

danger and with sadness. It is the winter equinox. The festivals of all cultures at this time of year are meant to bring light to the darkness of winter. This is what the Jesus myth is all about. The birth of hope. If winter comes, can spring be far behind. Or, as the poet Wallace Stevens wrote, "One must have a mind of winter to behold the junipers shagged with ice, and have been cold a long time, not to think of any sadness in the sound of the wind."

I have always had a mind of winter. I have always looked askance at the efforts people make to cheer themselves up. I think this is because I loved the preparations for Christmas so much, when I was a child, that the letdown when it was over was more than I could bear. Later, when I was part of a theatre group, the same thing would happen to me at the end of a play. We would be producing *Tiny Alice*, by Edward Albee, let us say. We would build a fabulous set, rehearse the play forty times, perform it ten times, then it would all be over. The curtain would fall, the audience would go home, we would read the reviews, fini.

The Christmases I most vividly remember took place during the Second World War, when my southern family was living in small towns in the midwest. My father was an engineer in charge of building airfields for the United States Air Corps. There was not much stuff in the United States during the Second World War. Most of the rubber and sugar and steel and gasoline and manufactured goods were being used to fight Germany and Japan. Everyone was a conservationist and a recycler. No one would have thought of wasting anything or complaining because there was no sugar. The only new household goods that we acquired for several years were black blinds to pull down during air-raid drills. I was very proud of those blinds and was reasonably sure they would keep my night light from guiding German bombers to Seymour, Indiana, but not certain that they would. I would have felt better if we could have taped them down with adhesive tape.

It was in this atmosphere that my eighth Christmas came.

For many weeks secrets were being kept in every corner of our small stucco house. My mother's beautiful cousin, Nell, whose husband had been killed in the war, was staying with us. Across the street our neighbors' house had a gold star in the window and a black wreath on the door. Their son had died somewhere in Europe. The neighbors on the other side had two sons in the navy. My brothers and I were the only children on the block.

I was making my older brother, Dooley, a book that had the schedules of all the nightly radio programs glued to the pages, along with some cartoons from the Sunday funny papers and a patriotic poem I had written. I was gluing the things to the pages with glue made from flour and water. While it worked well as an adhesive, it sometimes obscured part of the writing. I wasn't worried. Dooley and I knew the radio schedules by heart anyway. I knew that at six o'clock on Monday night *The Inner Sanctum* would come on, and I could either go on and listen to it and have bad dreams all night, or not listen to it and have dreams about a terrible story I imagined it telling. The theme of the stories was usually along the lines of MURDER WILL OUT.

So I was working on my present for Dooley and spending Saturday afternoons shopping at the five and ten cent store trying to decide what to buy my mother and my baby brother with the small amount of money I had saved from my allowance. I finally bought my mother a tiny little terra cotta planter made in Mexico. She still has it and keeps it proudly on a shelf beside her leather-bound editions of Shakespeare and Cervantes and Milton.

Dooley was keeping his door locked and giving me knowing looks. He knew it drove me crazy to keep secrets or have secrets kept from me. He knew that by the twenty-second of December I would start trying to cut deals with him, offering to tell him what I had for him in exchange for information about what I was going to get. I was pretty sure I didn't believe in Santa Claus but my parents were so adamant in their belief that I always began to waver as the time drew near.

The spirit of Christmas was so rich and strong that year even I was subject to its power. And with good cause. In the weeks preceding Christmas Eve, my mother and my cousin and the women in our neighborhood were preparing a surprise for me that I would remember all my life. In the dark of winter, in the darkest months of the Second World War, in the face of their mourning, these women were spending hours every night making me a doll's wardrobe the likes of which I have never seen again.

A wealthy contractor my parents had for dinner one night had sent my father a fabulous doll for me. He had thought I was cute I suppose, or else he was just as sad and burdened that winter as the rest of the United States. I remember his face the night he ate with us and the sadness in his hands and eyes as he talked to me. Perhaps I had shown him the book I was making Dooley. Perhaps he liked little messy red-headed girls who never combed their hair and slept with a night light to make up for listening to *Inner Sanctum*.

Anyway, he had mailed this fabulous doll to my parents to give to me, and my mother and her friends had decided to make a wardrobe for the doll. Out of the scraps of old clothes they had fashioned a complete wardrobe. There was a light blue wool coat trimmed with real leopard fur. There was a leopard hat. There was a nightgown with lace and a matching robe. There were knitted slippers and a dark red jersey dress for afternoons. There were aprons and a sunsuit. There were cotton underpants and several petticoats.

The doll had come dressed in a black and white checked taffeta evening dress and silk stockings and evening shoes. She had black hair and black eyes and little breasts and a lovely smile.

The other present I received was a toy washing machine with a wringer. It was an exact model of the one my mother had hooked up in the basement of the stucco house. When she used the machine it was my job to stand by with a broom to knock her down in case she got electrocuted.

At our house the children's presents from Santa Claus were

never wrapped up. They were left beside our stockings during the night, and as soon as we woke on Christmas morning we would run into the living room to see "what we got." My family was much too excitable to have a routine that was any more structured than that.

I slept in my room part of the night. Then I slept in-between my parents for a while. Then I slept on the foot of Dooley's bed, a boon that cost me five cents or ten poker chips on ordinary nights. Sometime during that night I may actually have been asleep for awhile. As I said, the spirit of Christmas was very powerful that year.

At dawn I ran down the stairs with Dooley right behind me. And there was the doll. She sat on my mother's slipcovered sofa in all her fabulous beauty. Her wonderful clothes were lying all around her. It was a present for a king's child. I could not even touch it. I could not even scream. Off to the side was the washing machine.

Dooley was running his hand up and down the barrel of a BB gun and watching me happily. He had known all along. Only eleven years old and he had been able to keep a secret of this magnitude.

My mother appeared with my father and my cousin behind her. I sat down on the floor and began to undress my doll. Off came the evening dress and the stockings and the shoes. On went the underpants, the jersey dress, the coat and hat. Off came the underpants and coat and hat and dress, on went the nightgown and the robe. This went on for half an hour while Dooley cocked and uncocked the BB gun and the baby woke up and was brought into the room and given his toys and my father read the Christmas cards from our distant relatives out loud. My mother went into the kitchen and made scrambled eggs and cinnamon toast with lots of rationed sugar. At ten o'clock I put my doll into a stroller and went to pay calls on the neighbors who had helped make the wardrobe. I strolled my doll from house to house. I went inside and had conversations and ate cookies and examined Christmas trees.

* * *

The day wore on into afternoon. My mother and father and the baby went to sleep for a nap. I played with my doll a while, then I had an idea. I took the toy washing machine down to the basement and set it up beside my mother's. I filled it with soap and water. I took the new doll clothes and began to stuff them into the washing machine. I was almost finished and was just stuffing in the blue wool coat with the leopard collar when my mother came down the stairs and found me. She began to cry. I had never seen my mother cry except at death but now she cried like a child. She didn't get mad. She didn't yell. She just began to take the precious clothes, now soaked in soap and water, and rinse them carefully in the sink, crying as she did so. "Don't worry," she was probably saying. "We will fix them. It will be all right." Of course it wasn't all right. Most of them would never be the same again.

But in the end it didn't really matter. What mattered were the hours the women spent making them. The wonderful surprise and the stupid, crazy thing I did that afternoon.

By January and February and March, as spring came and the tide of war turned in Germany, over their bridge tables and when they met on the sidewalk in the afternoons, the women began to tell the story. The more they told it, the funnier it became. It's still a pretty good Christmas story.

A Delta of Three Rivers

DRIVING IN the Delta in the early morning fog, pale yellow light, skies of clear blue above a thousand shades of green. Or, driving in the late afternoon, the sun spreading red beams across the land, or in November, when the picked cotton fields are rows of black crosses.

As I drive I pray for good weather for the farmers, picturing them driving into town to borrow money from the bank, in winter, with their ties knotted at the neck and their hats in their hands. So much depends on weather in the Delta but the rains usually come. Good weather is more usual than floods or drought in this blessed land.

My Delta is a flat alluvial plain that stretches from Greenville, Mississippi to Yazoo City. I drive through this country nine or ten times a year going from my home in Arkansas to the Mississippi coast where my grandchildren hold my heart hostage.

I have a three hundred mile drive before I reach the Delta, from the North Arkansas hills to the Arkansas Delta and across the Mississippi River on a bridge that is twenty miles from my mother's home. Then the heart of my journey begins. As soon as I cross the bridge, I turn onto Mississippi 454 and take a winding two lane road past a house built on top of an Indian mound. The mound is fifty feet high and still fat and strong after many years of carrying the house and withstanding rains. I continue on to Highway 1, the famous road that runs beside the levee. Beside the road are fields, then thick stands of trees, then the levee. Behind the levee is the Mississippi River, bringing rain and melted snow all the way from Minnesota. I love to drive beside the river. I was taught to think I was the richest girl in Christendom because I lived so near the river. The river belonged to us because we could go and look at its power and its beauty. My uncle lost an eye when he fell into it from a barge. My father and great uncle helped build the levee, my grandfather's farm had been flooded in the 1927 flood. Even a little fat, red-headed girl like me was part of the majesty of the river, simply from proximity. The British feel about their royal family the way people in the Delta feel about the river. There are smaller rivers and lakes and bayous where they fish and swim, but the Father of Waters is another thing.

By the time I have gone fourteen miles on Highway 1 and come to the turnoff into the Delta, I am a different person than the one who crossed the Greenville bridge. I become a child again in the delta, filled with the wonder of earth and sky and solitude. There will be very few cars or houses from now until I reach Yazoo City. I turn on Mississippi Highway 12 and the best part of the trip begins. For the next 34 miles I can drive a hundred miles an hour without endangering a soul, myself included. Many bugs will pay with their lives, and I will use up a tank full of window washing fluid but, aside from that, the worst thing that can happen is I'll have to slow down for a combine or go off into a cotton field. This land is as flat as a table top. The road is a straight line to Hollandale and then Belzoni. There used to be only cotton fields here, bordered by stands of hickory and oak, cypress and gum and holly and ash and elm, reminders that this land was all woods until white and black men followed the Indians and began to clear the trees. Now there are also rice and soybean fields and catfish ponds, rectangles of brown water surrounded by wildlife, cranes and flocks of egrets like white tulips. They are fat, happy birds, living on easy pickings, ponds brimming with captive fish. A man I know who works for the Fish and Game Commission has been trapping beavers for the farmers in the Delta. He caught a beaver last year that weighed ninety pounds from feeding on rice and soybeans. I wonder how big the egrets will become now that they don't have to do a thing but catch fish in catfish ponds.

The most beautiful sight is the rice fields. In spring they are a green that equals the sky for beauty. They are sheets of green silk unfolding in the wind. Think how gorgeous this must be to people who depend on rice for food.

We depended on cotton, which is why I love to watch it grow. But mostly I just love the drive. Just because I can drive a hundred miles an hour through this country doesn't mean I always do it. Sometimes I slow down to eighty and enjoy the view. Sometimes I stop at Leroy Percy State Park and walk in the woods and search for four leaf clovers.

I used to tell my editor I thought the reason people in New York City were depressed was because they never got to drive, or, if they did, it was always in heavy traffic with cursing and bad air. "We could make a million dollars," I used to tell him, "by flying people to the Delta to drive on the flat, straight roads. We could send in crop dusters to race them along the fields."

This is not a journey for listening to the radio or thinking about your troubles. This is a drive for pretending you are Master of the World. One warning. Don't stop the car and get out unless you are covered with insect repellant. The mosquitos will bite you anywhere. My trapper friend was bitten *in the ear*. I have been bitten on the legs through thick tights. Delta mosquitos will remind you it is a joke to think man is the top of the food chain.

I have never seen a highway patrolman on these roads. Keep your fingers crossed that one doesn't read this article and decide to spoil the fun.

A Journey to New York City

A TRIP becomes a journey when there is a destination. Our destination was the Egyptian Galleries at The Metropolitan Museum of Art in New York City. My oldest grandson is very interested in history. He is especially interested in Ancient Egypt. What thirteen year old worth his salt wouldn't be? Great stone tombs rising from the desert, secret hieroglyphs, mummies and golden treasures.

I had been longing to take him and his sisters to see the museum, but I was daunted by the thought of three children in New York City, the cost, the logistics, the danger.

This unfilfilled desire to show them my favorite city grew and festered in my brain. It got to the point where I could not enjoy museums anymore. They are thirteen and ten and eight years old. Perfect ages for great museums. Every thing I saw I would imagine through their eyes.

Then one night last October they called to read me their six week grades. They had made straight A's. All three of them had made straight A's. That was it. The time had come. I got their mother on the phone. I asked her if we could take them out of school for two days the following week. And would she come with us. She said yes to both questions so I called American Airlines and asked them to find us some tickets I could afford.

Luckily the children live in a small town on the Mississippi coast. The nearest airport is Gulfport, Mississippi and the mid-week flights to LaGuardia were wide open. By ten that night I had four non-refundable discounted tickets on their way to the coast. We were past the point of no return. Those children were going to see a bigger world. Or, at least, one that is dirtier and more populated and has better museums. *We will be making memories*, I told myself. *But there's no telling what they'll turn out to be.*

The following Wednesday afternoon we were on our way. Marshall, age thirteen, Ellen, age ten, Aurora, age eight, Rita, age forty, and yours truly, pushing sixty. Here are some scenes from the next five days. These are the things I will always remember.

In the sculpture garden of The Museum Of Modern Art, while the rest of us were gazing into the beautiful shallow pond by the Giacometti, Aurora climbed up on the Picasso goat and began to ride. A little black girl climbed up behind her. A man began to photograph them. Two well-dressed docents let out a scream. They went running toward the scene with their hands up in the air. We ran that way too. We converged around the goat. We stood in a circle telling the children to get down. We all apologized to each other. Still, I couldn't help thinking, *I have never appreciated Picasso until this*

moment. Two beautiful little girls sitting on his goat are probably a lot closer to what he envisioned than a lot of middle-
aged ladies with their hands up in the air.

As many times as I have been in that sculpture garden I had
never really noticed that goat. It is an entirely evil-looking
goat. It stood there, it's evil eyes surveying our distress. Above
the garden were huge gray clouds of many colors, gray and
white and stone and porcelain and granite and black and ivory.
"Those clouds contain water from the North Atlantic Ocean,"
I told my granchildren. "In those clouds is the breath of seals
and moisture that was once in icebergs."

"They are the color of the goat," Ellen said. "Clouds and
sculpture look alike, especially in the water."

"Naguchi would have loved it," Rita added. The women
warmed at that, and we all smiled and turned away.

That was a day that had begun with croissants and orange
juice and coffee on a bench in Central Park. Then a long walk
down Fifth Avenue to see the Plaza Hotel, scene of *Home Alone
II,* one of the children's favorite movies. At first I rebelled at
the thought of retracing the steps of a character in a movie,
then I lightened up and took them, not once, but twice, to
visit the lobby of The Plaza and look at the elevators and
chandeliers. Art and beauty civilize and make clear. They are
as welcome in a movie or a hotel lobby as in a museum. It was
good for me to be reminded of that before I turned into a lady
with her hands permanently in the air.

We left the Plaza and made a cursory trip to F.A.O.
Schwartz, which is across the street from the Plaza. Then
we continued down Fifth Avenue to my favorite store,
Steuben Glass. For years I had promised myself that I could
buy a piece called *The Sword in the Stone* as soon as I sold a
book. I have sold twelve books in that time and still have
not bought the sculpture. It has assumed a strange place
in my mind. It is a symbol of things I don't have to own
to enjoy. I am content to go and look at it when I'm in
New York City.

Aurora did not share my Puritan feelings. She was so touched by the beauty of the pieces that finally she grabbed my legs and said, "We should get one of these. Why can't we have one of these things?"

That afternoon her mother hailed a taxi and took her to Chinatown where there are things she can afford. She bought a ring with glass diamonds in it and a pair of sunglasses that make her look like Mata Hari.

But what of the Egyptian galleries? The destination that was to make this trip into a journey? We went to see them on the first morning we were there. We woke in a beautiful suite of rooms at The Westbury Hotel on Madison and Sixty-ninth. We dressed and had breakfast and walked down Fifth Avenue to The Metropolitan Museum of Art, which I think is the most exciting museum in the world.

We stopped at the fountain and let Rita take our photograph. Then we walked up the stairs and into this miraculous place where they collect and care for the wonders of the ages. We bought tickets and spent a few minutes with the Greek and Roman statues, then I took my grandson's hand and led him to the tombs of the Pharoahs.

"Awesome," he said, and then was strangely quiet as we visited the burial chambers, the giant sarcophagi, The Temple of Dendur, the mummies, and the scrolls of heiroglyphics. "I have read about these things," he said later. "But it is different when you see them in person."

"Do they seem smaller than you imagined?" I asked.

"No, they seem bigger." We shook our heads and looked into each other's eyes. It is not possible to say in words the force of these powerful stone relics of the past. Either they speak to your imagination or they don't. I had known that he would get it, and he did.

The weather was devine. It was the first week in November, and I had expected it to be freezing. In order to go to the city when it wasn't crowded with tourists I had decided bad weather would be worth it. I had even brought along an extra suitcase of gloves and hats and sweaters since these southern children do not need such things where they live. Instead it was constant sunshine and seventy degrees.

"No one in New York speaks English," my red-headed granddaughter Ellen, noted. "And none of them have red hair."

"I'll show you redheads," I told her. "We'll be on the lookout for them." After that I began to notice the diversity of the city. I have been there so much on business in the last few years that I have forgotton to use my eyes and ears for the real wonders of the city. We had Italian waiters, German hotel managers, Haitian taxi drivers. We had our hair cut by an Italian; we met a French family in the hotel elevator; we saw three beautiful Norwegians crossing a street in their brilliant knitted sweaters. At breakfast one morning we sat by an Oriental mother with a small child so perfect she took Aurora's breath away. "She's a perfect little doll," Aurora said. "She's the prettiest thing I've ever seen."

Twice people cried. My daughter-in-law cried at Monet's *Lilies*.

"Why are you crying?" Ellen asked.

"Because it is so beautiful," she answered. After that the children and I went off and left her alone to look at paintings. The four of us went to the American wing and sat on a bench looking at *Group of Bears* and the Tiffany windows. We held hands and hugged each other and tried to explain to Aurora why she is not allowed to climb the marble stairs carved with dancers that sits in the middle of a bed of ivy.

Later, on the last afternoon we were in New York, we came upon a copy of *Group of Bears*, in a playground in the park, and Rita photographed us climbing on it. Perhaps the reason to take children to the city is to teach them what to climb and what to leave alone.

On the second morning we were there, I took Ellen on a sentimental journey. We went to Elizabeth Arden to get our hair cut. When my mother and my aunts were young women, they would go together to New York City to see plays. They would spend the first morning they were in town at Elizabeth Arden. I always think of them when I enter that red door. I think of them emerging at noon, perfected, ready to go and see *My Fair Lady* or *Oklahoma* or *Brigadoon*. They would bring home the long-playing albums from those musicals, and I would listen to them all summer and memorize the lyrics. Those were the days, although the ones I am living are good enough for me. Walking down Fifth Avenue with my oldest granddaughter to have our hair cut into matching ultra-chic short hairdos is something I will not need a photograph to remember. We emerged from the red door into the bright lovely sunshine and walked along the avenue giggling and looking at ourselves in store windows. We went to Trump Tower and rode up and down on the escalators and said, "I love your hair," and "I love yours too," about a dozen times.

There are other fine memories. In The Museum of Modern Art, Aurora began to have the urge to paint. The next morning we went to an artists supply store and bought pastels and drawing paper and everyone drew and painted on the plane flying home.

There was a wonderful moment in a restaurant when Aurora didn't want anything to eat. It turned out she was lonesome for her school cafeteria. I left the restaurant and went to a deli and bought her a can of potato chips. "She is hungry for her native foods," I told the Korean waiter when I returned. "She needs contact with her native earth."

We went to bookstores and record stores. We went to an athletic shoe store and bought Nikes and rubbed elbows with people in town for the marathon. We walked in the park and saw the castle. We went to The Museum of Natural History and marveled at the dinosaurs and saw the free movie twice. We *worked* the city from eight in the morning until eight at night. There were many things we left undone. We didn't see the Statue of Liberty and I regret not taking Marshall to Yankee Stadium, where, he reminded me, Babe Ruth hit his hundredth home run. But that has always been the wonder of New York City. You can not exhaust its possibilities in a thousand visits. You always leave things half-finished and undone. There is a table in the Egyptian Galleries that contains a handkerchief that is the first clue that led to finding King Tut's tomb. A curator of the museum drew me a map to it so I could take Marshall and show him that and in the excitement of the morning I forgot to do it.

I'm Not Slave Material

"YOUR CHILDREN are not your children. They are the sons and daughters of life's longing for itself," wrote Kahlil Gibran. How he knew this is marvelous to me, since I have striven so long and hard to learn it. The rules I discovered while raising my own three sons are simple. You have to let them go. You have to let them ride off on their bikes when they are seven, and you have to stop giving them money and advice when they are 21. Of course, as long as you are giving them money you will think you have the right to give them advice. They will resent the advice. If you raised them, it won't be a thing they haven't thought of for themselves.

Nothing that you say now will help. They have to find their manhood. They have to forge their sword. Alone in the forest, like Siegfried, with only the broken pieces of his father's sword for material, they must forge the weapon they will use to kill the dragons of the world. It is very difficult to believe that they are capable of doing this. You must try to see the face of a grown man before you, not the face of the child you taught to tie his shoelaces.

I make it a point to live far away from both my parents and my children. If I lived near my parents I would be sucked into the morass of family problems which is the bread and water on which my parents thrive. They have partaken of this food for so long they think it's nectar. On the other hand, if I lived near my grandchildren I would become their slave. And I'm not slave material.

I believe that the greatest gift I can give my children is to have a life of my own that is not dependent on them. When they come to visit, they come of their own free will, not because they think I need them.

I try not to ask my children too many questions. Every question that a parent asks a child is a leading question. I try not to compare them to other people. And I am trying to learn not to be proud of them. The thing I am proud of today may be the thing they need to stop doing tomorrow in order to grow and change.

I am trying to learn to love them unconditionally, and this is where the money comes in. Giving money to a grown child is giving him power without responsibility. It will keep you from ever having a peer relationship with your child. A relationship where nobody gives advice or hovers or nags. In a peer relationship two people of equal worth and intelligence discuss the world *outside themselves*. They meet as equals and part without sorrow, trusting each other to return with good news. If I'm not paying for it, if it isn't going to cost me money, I can listen to their wildest plans with enthusiasm and respect.

Most of all I want to learn to trust in the future, which is always full of surprises. I am fiercely independent. So is my father. He is 85 years old, and last month, for the first time in our lives, I was able to do something for him that he couldn't do for himself. I went to visit my parents and found him trying to read a book with a plastic sheet of magnifying material he had ordered from a magazine. He is a constant reader. If he isn't working or plotting to control somebody's life, he is reading. In the last few years much of his reading has been about groups who are plotting to control the world. What he reads is not my business. His failing vision is another matter. He had just received word from a third doctor that it was impossible to operate and let more light into his eyes. So he was struggling away with the magnifying sheet and not complaining.

Luckily I had known a lawyer with a similar problem and had seen the marvelous magnifying instruments his wife had found for him.

I left the house on some flimsy excuse and spent the afternoon combing Jackson, Mississippi, for magnifying devices. Finally, in a mall, in a German instruments store, I found it. A raised, lighted rectangle that sat upon the page and made up for the light lost to the retina. I took it home and gave it to him. It was a great moment for me. The next month, in Paris, I found an even better device that fits into the palm of the hand and can be moved more easily across the page. I had it wrapped and shipped to him with a bottle of Guerlain's L'Heure Bleue for my mother.

There was a message on my answering machine from him when I came home last night. In his kind, cultured, vastly humorous, sweet Southern voice it said, "Sister, I was just calling to thank you for that nice, sophisticated reader you got, and I liked the perfume I was putting on myself too. Ten, four."

A long time ago we had metaphors for all that I have said. Push them out of the nest. Cut the apron strings. These are vast metaphors. Even more important now that we live such long lives. Plenty of time to create real relationships with the ones we kicked out, or the ones we wish had kicked us out a whole lot sooner.

Like a Flower of Feathers or a Winged Branch

THIS IS Pedro Calderon de la Barca's description of a bluebird. I read this one morning in a doctor's office and have thought of it daily ever since. Every time I see a bird or a branch of leaves or a flower I think of it.

This is the job of writing, to carve indelible metaphors into the mind of a reader. Can't you see, the writer must tell the reader. It is all one thing. Look outside yourself and see that we are all fashioned of the same forms, the seven basic forms of crystals. Look outside yourself. Look at me.

If that is the task, how can the writer achieve it? I think it is like building a wall. Let us suppose that the beginning writer is a man living alone on a piece of land. He wants to build a wall to keep other people from coming onto his land, but he has no tools or knowledge. All he knows is that he wishes to construct a barrier. He collects what he finds lying around, leaves and fallen branches. He stacks these things up. The first wind blows them away.

He finds stones and begins to make piles of them but they are heavy and cumbersome and in short supply, so he soon gives that up. Then he travels to the next piece of land and finds a man who is making bricks out of clay and stacking them up. Our man likes that idea. He goes home and makes a wall of clay bricks, but the spring rains melt the bricks and the wall tumbles.

He meets a third man who is making bricks and letting them dry in the sun before he stacks them up. Our man is very excited by this idea. He goes home and works twice as hard as before. He doesn't care how hard it is to do; now he will make a wall that will hold.

As he works day after day and week after week fashioning the bricks and setting them out in the sun to dry, he begins to imagine a wall so beautiful that other men will come to see it and marvel at its beauty. He begins to make each brick exactly the same size, with sides carefully trimmed. He notices the clay from the banks of his creek makes more beautifully colored bricks than the clay near his campfire. He begins to make long trips to bring back this thicker, redder clay. Now he doesn't like the dun colored bricks he made to begin with. He discards them. He is excited. He has lost his sense of time. He barely remembers to eat. He is going to make the most beautiful wall in the kingdom, the longest and the tallest and the most beautiful. Every day he gets up and works on the wall. He is a happy man. He has forgotten why he is building a wall. He has forgotten that he thought there was something that needed walling in or walling out. He is an artist with a plan and materials and skills. He has become a builder.

My life as a writer has been like that man making that wall. I have forgotten what I wanted from this work. I have never liked celebrity or having people ask me questions. Aside from being paid so I can go on writing there is nothing the outside world gives me in exchange for my writing that is of value to me. I do not take pleasure in other people's praise and I don't believe their criticism.

I love to make up characters and make things happen to them and then make them strong enough to survive their problems and go on to happy times. "Happy trails to you," I say to my characters at the end of my stories. I nearly always let my characters have happy endings because I wish that for myself and for my readers. I don't want to send my readers to bed with sad or malignant endings.

Pedro Calderon de la Barca lived in Spain in tragic times. His father was a tyrant and the only woman he ever loved died in childbirth. She died giving birth to Caleron's illegitimate child. Because of these things Calderon was forced to have a tragic view of life. He was concerned with guilt. He believed that a man can be responsible through his own wrongdoing for the wrongdoing of another. That the greatest sinner is also the most sinned against. These are deeply tragic beliefs, and yet the poetry with which Calderon expressed these beliefs was so beautiful that it has lasted all these years.

Like a flower of feathers or a winged branch. That is what we want to write. But first we must learn to make a wall. We must find what materials are available to us and we must learn to shape them and we must forget what we were doing it for. If you get lonely, and it is lonely work, invoke the spirits of past artists to stand by you and teach you by their examples. Today, for me, it is Don Pedro Calderon de la Barca, poet and playwright, born January 17, 1600, Madrid, Spain, died, May 25, 1681, Madrid.

The Fabulous Booklined Walls of My Grannie

SHE LIVED IN A small wooden house on the main street of Courtland, Alabama, and the walls of her house were lined with books. In many ways I suppose she was the town librarian since people came there to read and borrow books and sit on the porch and talk about books. Everything was censored in the 1940s so little children could sit on the swings and listen to anything that was being said. They could also read anything on the walls and not be in danger of having their minds

corrupted. When I was alone with her in that house our program was set. We spent the hot afternoons on beds reading
books and eating pound cake and drinking tea. The phone
never rang that time of day and no one came to visit. Even the
animals and birds were quiet, waiting for evening. If it was
summer, the magnolia trees would be so full of blooms they
perfumed the town. Magnolia, honeysuckle, and jasmine
mixed with dust from the roads and the DDT we sprayed on
the cotton to keep the bugs from eating the bolls.

If the books we were reading were particularly mesmeriz-
ing our reading might go on until bedtime. If one of us was
completely immersed in a book, the other one understood.
When I was young, I would be reading the Campfire Girls or
Tarzan books or anything about camping. Later I would be
reading Thomas Costain or Lloyd C. Douglas or Kathleen
Winsor. She would be reading Irving Stone or anything about
Scotland. When we were reading, we liked each other. She
never fixed elaborate meals and expected me to eat them when
I was in the middle of a chapter. I never asked her to do anything for me. I liked to make my own sandwiches or eat bread
and butter and that was fine with her. When we were reading,
we were in perfect accord. I wonder if she knew how lucky she
was to have a granddaughter who shared her love of books.
Alas, I don't think she did. She liked boys better than she
liked girls and I knew it and this was a shadow that lay between us. Also, she had said on many occasions that I was impossible. I was impossible and intended to stay that way. She
was impossible too, which was her charm for me. No matter
how hard I tried I could not get that woman to act like she
loved or approved of me.

There we were, reading books about English and Scottish
queens, about heroines who rode like men and were more
stubborn than any of the men they loved. There we were, as
alike as we could be and all that either of us saw was each
other's stubbornness. It was a battle neither of us would ever
win.

The summer I was eight years old was the first time I stayed with her alone for any length of time. I was already a dedicated reader by then, so I was looking forward to being in her house full of books. Still, I was accustomed to having my way, to running roughshod over my sweet, southern mother, and this Grannie was a different adversary. She didn't like craziness or give in to threats or act like she was afraid I was going to fall out of trees. She didn't react. Like a great lawyer she could watch and wait and keep her counsel until time to strike.

The summer I was eight the main argument between us was over my clothes. What I would wear when I got up in the morning and began my daily business of climbing every tree in Courtland, Alabama and making nests in them. I had a main lookout in the old mimosa that leaned into the porch and a second post in a hundred year old magnolia in the side yard. Old magnolia trees are covered with a black residue which coats anything it touches. I was up there a lot, looking like a chimney sweep when I came down. I also climbed any other tree I saw. If a tree had branches I could reach I climbed it.

I had brought with me to Courtland a large, leather suitcase filled with beautiful dresses my maternal grandmother had made for me. My mother's side of the family loved girls and adored dressing them up and looking at them. These clothes had to be ironed and my grandmother in Courtland didn't have anyone around to iron clothes all day. After a few days of my coming down out of trees in ruined clothes she called a dressmaker. That afternoon the woman appeared. She was a sad, middle-aged woman who came into the house carrying bolts of blue and white and brown and white striped seersucker. She spread the material out across the sofa. "That's ugly," I said. "I won't wear that."

"Don't be rude," my grandmother answered. "Apologize to Mrs. Marks."

"Well, I won't wear anything made out of that. It looks terrible. It looks all wrinkled."

"Just let me make you one and see if you like it," Mrs. Marks put in. "It will be pretty when it's made up. I'll put rick-rack on it." She had struck a chord. I loved rick-rack. As a practiced child mannequin in my mother's world, I knew all about fabrics and trim and buttons and patterns.

"All right," I agreed. I took off my ruined white dress and dropped it on the floor. I had been in the mimosa playing Tarzan when Grannie called me in to meet Mrs. Marks.

I stood as still as I could while Mrs. Marks pinned a paper pattern on me. I was beginning to like her. She was patient and gentle and didn't stick me with a pin.

Two days later the playsuits appeared. She had made one from each bolt of cloth. A blue and white one and a brown and white one. They had straps which buttoned onto a sleeveless bodice. The bottoms were large, loose shorts. "I won't wear that," I declared. "I'd look like some kind of dwarf. I'd look like a freak at the fair."

"The pants are a bit baggy," Mrs. Marks agreed. "I can take them in."

"It won't do any good," I said. "I'm still going to hate them. I won't put them on."

Mrs. Marks pulled the cloth of the pants into a ball at the back. She pulled and pinned and knit her brow. All I did was shake my head. My Grannie sat on the sofa with her mouth set in a line.

Mrs. Marks removed the offending playsuit from my body. She packed up her seersucker and left. Grannie followed her out onto the porch and put her hand on her shoulder. They were deep in conversation. They were plotting against me, but I was not worried. No one had ever made me wear anything I didn't want to wear. There had been epic battles over starched dresses and seams that itched and sleeves that touched me. I had never lost a battle, and I wasn't going to lose one now.

My grandmother returned to the living room. "Let's have

some tea and toasted biscuits," she suggested. "Then we can read for a while." She went into the kitchen to boil the water and I wandered to a wall and began to read the titles of the books. Every title was a wonder in itself. The physical reality of the books was part of my love for them. The frayed dust jackets, the red and blue and green bindings. The wonderful ideas of the titles. Every title an invitation to a world. I would take books down and read a page or two until something hooked me. Sometimes I started reading in the middle and finished the book before I read the beginning. I still do this occasionally. Great writing allows you to begin anywhere.

My grandmother in Courtland had gone to college in Kentucky before she married my grandfather. There was a photograph of her on her dresser in her cap and gown when she graduated. I had heard about women who were bluestockings. I was pretty sure I was going to be one, but it didn't scare me. I would look at that photograph of my grandmother and wonder if she was a bluestocking too.

"Ellen," she called out from the kitchen. "Come and have your tea." She was waiting, presiding over her simple painted kitchen table. It was set with silver and handmade placemats. There were linen napkins. We were having tea and toasted biscuits and butter and milk and honey.

"The reason I want you to wear the playsuits is three-fold," she began, pouring my tea. "First it is because when you are in trees people can see your underpants. You are too big to let people see your underpants. If you want to be up in a tree it is fine with me, but you must be dressed like an adventurer, not an actress."

"Yes, ma'm," I said, and put some butter on a biscuit.

"The second reason is the war effort," she continued. "Every one in town is working at the air force base. There is no one left over to iron your dresses. Seersucker is a very patriotic fabric. It's easily washed, dries quickly, and does not have to be ironed. Also, since it is striped, it will serve as camouflage. If you are playing army in the trees, as I saw you doing the other day with Sykes Martin, it would be very good to have on a playsuit that is striped and hard to see in the leaves."

"Okay," I said. I was weakening. "I might wear the blue ones. But not the brown ones."

"There is one more thing." She put her teacup down into her saucer and fixed me with her brown eyes. "Mrs. Marks lost a son in the war. What's more she is a widow. She is very proud and working as hard as she can to support herself and forget her grief. It would be a bright spot in her life if she saw you going up a mimosa in her creation. On the other hand, if you are rude when she returns with them, she will feel she has failed me and as we are friends that will cause her pain."

I was silent. The burden of this conversation was too much to bear. So much depended on me. It was like the time the headhunters had Nyoka tied to the tree. It was like the little boy who had to keep his finger in the dyke.

"I will wear the blue ones," I said. "Maybe I will wear the brown ones. Maybe not."

"All right. Thank you." She leaned across the table and put honey on my biscuit. She did not gloat. She did not keep talking about it.

"I will wear them," I added. "If you'll pretend to think the little people are in the radio when we go to bed tonight."

"Then we'll have to go to bed on time. Otherwise I'll fall asleep while I'm talking."

It was my favorite thing any grown person had ever done but it was usually impossible to get her to do it unless she was in the mood. She would occasionally go into marvelous inventive moods in which she would pretend outlandish things, but you could never get her to repeat a performance on command.

Later that night, when we were in bed with the lights out and the radio on she did it. "Let them out of there," she began in a falsetto voice. "Please let those little people out of that box. They've been in there for days. Open the door. Please let them out. They need to go home and go to bed."

"They have to stay until they finish the program," I said, then I dissolved in laughter. For some reason this was the funniest thing on earth to me. She kept on pretending to be this very dumb country woman who didn't know how the radio worked and in between convulsing with laughter, I explained to her as best I could what a radio was and why it was plugged in and where the voices were coming from.

As a poem she taught me when I was older says, "Where is she now, for whom I carry in my heart, this love, this praise."

I've Always Meant to Tell You

Dearest Mother,

I want to thank you for the beautiful blue and white cups you sent me on my sixtieth birthday. For the blue linen napkins and the white placemats. I want to thank you for introducing me to blue. The cobalt blue of your beautiful English eyes. It must have been the first thing I ever saw. Smiling down at me as they have been for all my sixty years. Thank you for not dying. Here I am, sixty years old and I have never had to grieve for deep or tragic loss. That's what your death would be to me. Imagine not being able to call 601 956 2348 and tell you my troubles. I tell you my troubles to take your mind off your own. I never told you that, did I? It's a secret I've been keeping for about twenty years. You are twenty-seven years older than I am and your troubles are harder than mine are, so I always call and tell you about my allergies and my back and neck and insect bites. Everyone knows there is nothing wrong with me. I pretend to be a hypochondriac in order to deliver messages to you. The message is, our bodies heal themselves.

Thank you for the powerful healthy genes. Tomorrow the sun will be shining and we will be like new. I know you. Every morning you think the world is beginning all over and all will be well in the world. I think so too. Where do you think I got an idea like that?

But mostly the thing I keep forgetting to tell you is how much I love the aesthetic that you gave me. I travel a lot. I run into my distant cousins, in California and New York City and Colorado. There they are, with those blue eyes and that darling nose, wearing Chanel Nineteen and dressed in simple, elegant, tasteful clothes. "Your necktie rich and modest, but asserted by a simple pin." I used to think it was funny that I can't talk myself into being tacky. I used to try. I would go out and buy outlandish clothes or shoes or think of painting something red but I could never carry it off. I like blue and navy blue and black and white and yellow. The way you dressed me when I was a child.

I want rooms simple and clean and quiet, with a bowl of fresh roses or lilies on a table. Not two bowls of flowers. One bowl of flowers. I don't want to outdo anyone. I want to make things that people think are beautiful and let them look at the things I make. When I write I want to solace and amuse my readers. Sometimes I want to shock them into being solaced. I didn't learn that from you. I know I have a hit on my hands when you call me up after I have written a book and tell me, Ellen, this is filthy. If you knew how much I love it when you say that, you would never do it.

Do you know where cobalt blue comes from? Our favorite color. It was brought to China from Turkey by the Chinese traders on the Silk Road. They discovered the cobalt tiles in the temples of Turkey and brought it back just in time for the Ming dynasty. I love those cups you gave me for my sixtieth birthday. I drink coffee out of them each morning. I put one in each bathroom in my house. I put those beautiful white placemats on the table and those blue linen napkins and eat dinner in the heart of the civilization you passed on to me.

I am sorry you are growing old and have to have your knee operated on and put up with the long recovery. I'm sorry that it takes so long for cuts to heal. But I never say this to you. I call you up the minute you get back from the hospital and start telling you my problems. A girl with a mother like you should have better manners than that. A girl with a mother like you should know how to exhibit sympathy. Instead, I do it the way I have always done it when you were sick or injured. I call 601-956-2348, and, as soon as you answer, I say, "Hello, my mother. This is me."

"How are you?" you immediately ask.

"Well, my allergies are better but I've had to go to the chiropractor about a hundred times this week for my neck. You should see my cherry tree. There are five million cherries on it and about a thousand birds. There are twenty different species in that tree. There are redbirds and bluebirds and blue jays by the dozens. There is a piliated woodpecker the size of a dinosaur. How are you? How's your leg?"

You know me like a book. I can't fool you. You know what I am saying, don't you? Like you know how much it pleases me when something I write shocks you. Scares and pleases me. In your presence I am not a writer. I am a hyperactive, red-headed child whom it is your duty to love and civilize.

You don't know how you have civilized me. You will never know how much you've taught me and how deep the lessons go. I think you know I love you. I know that you love me.

Don't die. Love, Ellen

(Note to young writers. I woke up dreaming this essay. If I stay
alone long enough, I will always begin to write. It is the
imaginary playmate syndrome. I don't know who I was writing this essay about my father to. Probably my next door
neighbor, whose father died last week. He was also a Scotch
Presbyterian and a man who lived a long time because he
hated and feared to die. What a great honesty was in my
daddy. He was a fierce and brave man. Of course he didn't
want to die. Who does?)

My father's father was a famous hunter and horseman in
North Alabama, who loved to take his silver and his servants
and go out and live in the woods. Because of this everyone in
our family was taught to live in the woods, to make fires and
leave trails and know where to camp and what to do if they
were lost. I carried a compass with me at all times from the
age of six to twelve although I was never sure I really knew
how to use it.

My brother probably really knew how to use the compass.
Anyway, at some point he and my father began to go off camping without me. They had tired of my constant complaining
and wanted to go deeper into the woods and stay longer. At
about age eight, they stopped inviting me on their expeditions,
and my camping education was turned over to the wonderful
summer camps my father found for me to go to. The first great
camp was in Ohio. Columbus Girl's Camp. Months before I was
to go there, Daddy brought a small black trunk into my room,
and we began to pack it. There was a list the camp had sent of
things I was to bring and we followed it exactly. Two small
sheets, a pillow, a wool blanket, six pairs of socks, six pairs of
underpants, three pairs of shorts, a pair of long pants. Every

morning when I would awake, I would see the trunk sitting at the foot of my bed, a promise of great things to come.

My father died three years ago this week. It was two years after his death before I could bear to have a photograph of him in my house. I had his Auburn tie hanging in a back closet with the black gown I wore to receive an honorary doctorate from Millsaps College, one of the few important events of my life that he attended. He was not a public man. He was a man to take a little girl off alone and teach her to make a fire. He was a man to load five children into a pickup truck after the first long freeze and take them off to spend Saturday clearing a pond for ice skating. He was a man to buy enough ice skates for every child in the neighborhood who could not afford a pair. He was a man who could create huge excitement out of nothing.

He would come home from a hard week's work carrying a box full of long underwear and ice skates, and by Saturday morning at nine we would be in the truck going to find a pond. We were living in Mound City, Illinois, but we were from the deep south. None of us knew how to ice skate, including my father, but he was a great athlete and he had been asking questions of the people he worked with. Also, he had found a farmer who would lend us his pond. It would be my father, my seven year old brother, me, aged five, and three other children in the neighborhood. There were never any other girls along on these expeditions but that was a way of life for me, as all of my cousins were boys. The only time there were girls was when we were horseback riding. My father's grandmother had been a famous horsewoman in North Alabama, and he approved of women riding horses.

When we had found the pond, we collected firewood and built huge fires on both ends of the pond. Then we took two by fours out of the truck and began to push them across the ice, smoothing it down for skating. Nothing was ever simple with my father. Everything he thought up to do included hard work. The ideal was Sonya Henie and the little Dutch boy who skated miles to save his city from disaster in a story book we had. The reality was pushing the two by fours across the pond and hauling brush to keep the fires going.

Finally we put on the skates. Then we stood up and began to learn to use them. To this day I can still go to an ice rink and put on skates and skate on them. The body does not forget skills it learned to save itself from falling. I am sixty-four years old now. When I was sixty-two, I was stuck in Tulsa, Oklahoma for twelve hours because of flight delays, and I took a taxi out to the indoor ice rink and rented skates to see if I could still skate on them. I wasn't Sonya Henie but I sure made it around the rink a few times.

I woke this morning thinking about my daddy and all the things he taught me to do. He was the most exciting person I have ever been around and the most exacting. I miss him greatly and I am glad my mind has decided to let my memories of him return. I have to go to New York City to talk to business people next week. I think I'll get out the Auburn tie and wear it to make me strong.

℞

THE REASON to write is to learn. The more I write, the more I am forced to learn. This winter I am having to study geology so that a teenage detective named Ingersol Manning can discover a map to a kimberlite pipe in Berkeley, California. A kimberlite pipe is the source of diamonds in the world. ". . . a relatively small hole bored through the crust of the earth by an expanding combination of carbon dioxide and water which rises from within the earth's mantle and moves so fast driving magma to the surface that it breaks into the atmosphere at supersonic speeds. Such events have occurred at random through the history of the earth, and a kimberlite pipe could explode under Moscow next year. Rising so rapidly and from so deep a source, a kimberlite pipe brings up exotic materials the likes of which could never appear in the shallow slow explosion of a Mt. St. Helens or the flows of Mauna Loa. Among the materials are diamonds."*

A kimberlite pipe is about a half a mile wide. If there is one underneath Ingersol's neighborhood, he and his friend, Tammili, and their mentor, the pianist, Mrs. Coleman, will have to decide whether it's worth telling anyone and having their neighborhood destroyed in the process.

Anyway, I had to study geology for many nights. Two things happened because of that, and both of them may prove to be irreversible. First, I have begun to view the world from an entirely different perspective. I live in the Ozark Mountains, soft, old hills left by glaciers ten million years ago and since then eroded and worn down by rain and snow and forests. I have always thought they were beautiful and always been fascinated by the huge rocks that seem to spring up from the earth. Everywhere there are boulders of many sizes still working their way to the surface. My house is built of that rock, much of it broken up from larger stones.

Now I can no longer look around me and see the spring trees and the soft, new grasses and wildflowers. Now all I see is geomorphic time, the long processes that brought that rock down here from Canada.

The basins, ridges, shelves, gullies, erosions, roadcuts, all have taken on huge, exciting lives. I am outside five hours a day exploring this and wondering and thinking. This is exciting work. This is an exciting life.

When I am through for the day I go to the bookstore and buy all the books on geology I can carry home. I have started giving them to children.

The reason I have become so excited about this subject is that I have found a use for it. I am a Scot. Most of the blood

*John McPhae

that runs in my veins came from County Cantyre, Scotland, and I don't like to waste things. If I can't see a practical use for something, sooner or later I get rid of it or give it away. I am using this geomorphic information to write a book that someday I might be able to sell, and that someday young people might read and be amused by, or learn something from. With that in mind, I began my study of geology with enthusiasm. It has developed into a passion. I have not yet bought a rock hammer and a set of cold chisels but that will be next. I did almost have a wreck on a mountain road last Wednesday. I came to a roadcut with a great fall of granite. I must have passed that place hundreds of times as it is on the main road south from my home. "Granite," I screamed. "Granite, granite, granite." I threw on the brakes and was almost rearended by a Highway Patrol car. Fortunately, the officer had been maintaining a proper distance and was able to swerve around me. I was preparing a defense in my mind, but he drove on and did not bother me.

The second thing this new passion has done for me is to bring me back to consciousness after a long winter's sleep. Three weeks ago I was so bored I was watching television. While watching The Learning Channel I became convinced that there had been an Atlantis and that it was now Anarctica. I talked of nothing else for days, boring all my friends to death. While buying the geology books I picked up Carl Sagan's *The Demon-Haunted World*, and was brought back to consciousness about pseudo-science, even when it's on The Learning Channel. There may have been a city in the Aegean that toppled into the sea, or was covered by an earthquake, but that is a far cry from "the destruction of a continent on which had sprung forth a preternaturally advanced technical and mystical civilization."

The reason to write is to learn. The red streaks on rocks are iron. We are made of stardust, you, me, this paper, your thoughts, dreams, and hammers. Your diamond rings and number two lead pencils. How blind we usually are. Not only to the real phenomena, which our five senses cannot see, but to the wonder that is here, beneath our feet, in Central Park, in every stone, the real history of the world, written in granite and marble and Feldspar and Dolomite and Gypsum and opals and rubies and diamonds. Diamonds enter the earth's surface at Mach 2. How's that for a birth process?

℘

FOR YEARS people have asked me why so many writers come from the south and for some reason that question has always annoyed me. It seemed obvious to me why writers come from the south, and yet, when I tried to articulate an answer, the answer was always lacking. No matter how many ideas I advanced, no matter how many theories I created, it wasn't enough.

"Why do so many writers come from the south?" the person would say, and I would see in my mind's eye the south I knew, the wonderful, mystical place from which my parents came and to which I was driven every summer so that I would not become a yankee even though we had to live in Indiana and Illinois until the United States won the Second World War and my father became rich enough to "go home."

The south I was driven to was a land of flat, delta fields and rooms full of people talking, talking, talking. Porches at night with people drinking whiskey and talking. Porches in the afternoon with women drinking tea and talking. Porches in the early morning with my grandmothers and great grandmothers and great aunts and great great aunts drinking coffee and talking. Kitchens full of people making mayonnaise and stirring batter for cakes and cornbread and talking. The cooks and I out in the garden picking vegetables for lunch and talking. People wearing starched shirts and dresses waiting around for church to start and talking. The minister preaching, the choir singing, us singing "A Mighty Fortress is Our Lord" and "The Church's One Foundation" and "I Sing a Song of the Saints of the Lord." Our voices everywhere, filling the earth with exclamations, excitations, questions, answers, pining, crooning, laments and praises.

Even if I were alone on the lawn inspecting bugs and collecting things the world was full of sound, crickets and birds and frogs and the wind, the sound of the bayou running past, voices rising from fishing boats, oars touching water, laughter from the store and the bridge, people teasing and upbraiding, stories being told, excitement passed along.

Of course we had to begin to write some of that down. If I think of the late afternoons when the houses were quieter I see in my mind's eye people reading and writing. The minute they stopped talking they began to read and write.

"Read to me," I was always demanding. I didn't want them to stop and read a *children's book*. I wanted to hear the essays in the *Progressive Farmer* or the letters to the editor in the *Deer Creek Journal* or the short stories in *The Reader's Digest* or *Good Housekeeping*, or, if it were my Great Grandmother Biggs or my Grandmother Gilchrist, some paragraphs from the latest Book of the Month Club book. I could go all over the house at Hopedale Plantation being read to. Eli Naylor might be in the kitchen reading Exodus or Leviticus, my brother, Dooley, would be reading *The Hardy Boys*. My cousin, Bunky, would be reading a *National Geographic*, my cousin, Laura, would be reading a musical score she was memorizing for the piano.

All we did was talk and read and write and sing. Of course we became writers. All my cousins believe they could write anything I write if they would agree to go live all alone in the Ozark Mountains and be too selfish to stay married. I believe it too but I never encourage any of them to do it.

If you are a child and you have an ambition to do something in the world, it is helpful if you know a real, live person who has already done it. Because there is a tradition of writing in the south and many writers live here, it is possible to have these "role models" without anyone noticing it or calling them that.

In my case I knew writers and I knew someone who knew a poet. My grandmother had gone to school with a poet named Mildred Plew Meigs and had an autographed copy of her book of poems to prove it. I was allowed not only to read this book of poems but to carry it around in my hand and take it to my room and dog ear the pages and finally, when I was older, to own it. No wonder I became a writer. I didn't think it was some mystical thing no human being could achieve. My grandmother had walked and talked with a real, live poet. This proved becoming a writer was within the grasp of mortal men.

Also, and equally important, my aunt was married to a newspaper editor. I would show off for him unmercifully whenever he came into a room. I wanted him to know we belonged to the same subspecies, that I was a writer too, although it hadn't been made manifest yet.

All of these answers seemed sufficient for my life and work, but they did not tell me why Richard Wright became a writer or Eudora Welty, whose parents were from the midwest.

* * *

A piece of the puzzle fell into my lap a few weeks ago and that piece is the inspiration for this essay. I was watching a documentary on Irish immigration and the announcer said the English settled the northeast but mostly Irishmen and Scots settled the south. Eureka! I screamed. It's a Celtic thing. Then I began to figure. I am half English, a quarter Irish and Welsh and a quarter Scots. The way I figure that is, the Scots blood makes me love to work, the English genes make me anal retentive about finishing what I start and the Irish and Welsh are the magic that turns words to music. I would bet there are very few southern writers without some Celtic genes but please don't get mad at me for believing that or challenge me to prove it. Many other racial groups have great musical and verbal skills. Perhaps it is the blend of all of that which has made us writers.

All of that is, of course, conjecture. What I know for sure is that southerners are writers because they love language and they love to live in worlds of their own making. Shakespeare loved the worlds he created. Harold Bloom says of Shakespeare he saved his creativity for the plays. He wasn't a wastral or a crazy man or mean to people. Everyone who wrote of him says he was a pleasant person who was fun to know.

William Shakespeare is my favorite writer. My second favorite writer is William Faulkner. I think he also loved the worlds he was creating. That's why he kept on writing about them until he died. He had to keep on finding out what was happening in Yoknapatawpha County.

When I was younger, I hated being called a southern writer. I wanted to be a universal writer. Now I know there never was a universal writer, just an occasional man or woman who was so true to the place they knew that it was made meaningful to people in any culture.

I was reading *The God of Small Things* last summer and I kept thinking, this is just like the Delta. A writer has hit pay dirt when the reader thinks the other side of the world is just like the place they lived.

It is all metaphor. Everything is a metaphor for everything else. Everything stands for everything else.

Wherever there are men and women and love and death and courage and kindness and betrayal there will be writers. Maybe there are so many southern writers because we have been living so hot and heavy down here for so many years. It took hot, passionate, powerful men and women to carve a civilization out of the wilderness of forest and swamp and plains that was the south. From the very beginning, from the time Cortez came from Florida to Arkansas, there were epidemics carried by mosquitos and many people dying along the way.

There were floods and plagues and forests to cut down and rivers to tame.

Later, by the time I got here, there were screened-in porches to keep out the mosquitos and time in the late afternoon to drink whiskey and tell the stories. I was lucky to live when that was going on and curious enough to listen. My mother was telling a story the other day about a friend of hers who married beneath herself and had "rough children."

Maybe that's why we are writers. Maybe we are a lot of rough children. Most of the southern writers I know would fit into that category, except, of course, Eudora, who is the exception that disproves everything I say.

Provenance

ORIGINS

INFLUENCES

WORK

PROVENANCE

*The author is grateful to the following for permission to reprint
previously copyrighted material:*

Excerpt from *The Dancing Wu Li Masters* by Gary Zukav. Copyright © 1979
by Gary Zukav. Reprinted by permission of William Morrow & Co. Ltd.

Excerpts from "Burnt Norton" and "East Coker" in *Four Quartets* by T. S.
Eliot, copyright 1943 by T. S. Eliot; renewed 1971 by Esme Valerie
Eliot. Reprinted by permission of Harcourt Brace Jovanovich, Inc. and
Faber & Faber Ltd.

Excerpts from the unpublished papers of Walter Inglis Anderson reprinted
by permission of the family of Walter Inglis Anderson.

Excerpt from "Renascence" in *Renascence & Other Poems* by Edna St. Vincent
Millay. Copyright 1917 by Edna St. Vincent Millay. Reprinted by per-
mission of Elizabeth Barnett, Literary Executor of the Estate of Edna St.
Vincent Millay.

Excerpts from "Letter Written on a Ferry While Crossing Long Island
Sound" in *All My Pretty Ones* by Anne Sexton. Copyright © 1962 by
Anne Sexton. Reprinted by permission of Houghton Mifflin Company.